The Olympics' 50 Craziest Stories

A Five Ring Circus

Les Woodland

McGann Publishing
Cherokee Village, Arkansas

Published by McGann Publishing
P.O. Box 576
Cherokee Village, AR 72525
USA
www.mcgannpublishing.com

**McGann
Publishing**

ISBN 978-0-9843117-8-1
Printed in the United States of America

Persians…inquired of [deserters from Arcadia] what the Greeks were doing. The Arcadians answered: "They are holding the Olympic games, seeing the athletic sports and the chariot races."

"And what," said the man, "is the prize for which they contend?"

"An olive wreath," returned the others, "which is given to the man who wins."

On hearing this, Tritantaechmes, the son of Artabanus, uttered a speech which was in truth most noble, but which caused him to be taxed with cowardice by King Xerxes. Hearing the men say that the prize was not money but a wreath of olive, he could not forbear from exclaiming before them all, "Good heavens, Mardonius, what manner of men are these against whom you have brought us to fight—men who contend with one another, not for money, but for honor."

Herodotus, The Persian Wars, VIII, 26

Table of Contents

Introduction

Five Ring Circus

It's such an odd idea: a school sports day on a global scale. Remember school sports days? That was when kids who hadn't the slightest interest, still less aptitude, were made to run and to hurl themselves or things about. Nobody but the sporty types who took these things seriously cared who won. They probably used their sack race or the under-14 discus to secure places in proper sports clubs. Or got grants to universities more interested in their brawn than their brain.

Nobody else cared. Except maybe for some of the parents who sat, dressed awkwardly as for a wedding, who felt they ought to attend.

"The result of the 80 meter dash is as follows..."

They'd listen attentively, some of them, consulting duplicated lists of events, but the rest had no more interest than did the spindly boys before them in cotton shorts. To the other parents, loudspeaker announcements were just another interruption to a forced conversation with the parents—or more usually just the mother, whom society would assume had less interest even than the father—sitting on wooden benches beside them.

"Oh, Mr. Johnson, you're my boy Johnny's geography teacher, aren't you?"

The geography teachers must have hated it just as much. Sports teachers are known in unkind schools as boneheads. The teachers of geography, physics, mathematics and languages see themselves as socially higher. A few, it's true, would also have played sports in their spare time. But even they could see the futility of making fat children run.

So, if nobody but the sporting swats enjoyed it, how did it come that the Olympics grew so large? Why were people prepared to die— well, perhaps not prepared to die but some did nevertheless—in their enthusiasm to win a ring of privet for their heads? Why do towns pay millions to put them on and, quite often, pay more millions in debt as the Games rolled on and left them behind?

Because, I suppose, we enjoy other people making an effort. It's so much more satisfying to watch and applaud than do it ourselves. We, who would have trouble reaching the end of a running track, feel free to criticize those who manage it in seconds but miss a medal by half the length of a leg.

I remember the British runner, David Bedford, when he returned to London after thousands of miles spent training and then a single race in which he'd run to his best but not won. The British, not the most violent of nations, turned on him. He was a disgrace to the nation according to sports journalists who had trouble lifting their bellies out of the chair.

And Ben Johnson. Not, it's true, the most honorable man in the world but probably not alone in cheating. The world which cheered when he ran 100 meters in 9.79 seconds spat at him in the street when it emerged he'd taken drugs to do it. But he'd still had to run 10.2 meters a second—which is 36.76 kilometers per hour from a standing start. About twice as fast as most people could manage on a bicycle.

To fix a race at 36.76 kilometers per hour, you have first to run at 36.76 kilometers per hour.

I remember when Britain did well in rowing one year. I didn't live there but friends who did sent me message bubbling at the news. Rowing... Whoopee! Suddenly a nation which knew nothing of rowing beyond the inter-university boat race along the Thames, and was no longer much interested in that, was passionate about rowing.

Why?

Because vicariously we see their success as our success. People say "Didn't we do well in the Olympics?" even when the closest they'd been was the other side of a television screen. We are pleased when we win. So pleased, that we have in the past given our winners free yogurt for life or offered them university doctorates. Or, conversely, we lost interest in them when they were no longer useful to us and we cared little when those we lauded died penniless and sometimes alcoholic in a slum.

Les Woodland

Well, this isn't a list of sporting achievements. Not in the sense of lists of runners and starters, of winners and losers. The times, the placings, are less interesting than the people who achieved them. For the Olympics is the school sports day that's churned out eccentricity and scandal, calamity and catastrophe.

It is a Five-Ring Circus.

It is the Olympic Games.

1

How To Be A Snooty Monarch

A strange old bird, Queen Wilhelmina. They thought the world of her in Holland, of course, but to the rest of the world she was a heavy, dumpy woman, a queen who made a dent in the throne. She wasn't the first person to whom you'd lend a bicycle. Her father was 63 when she was born, which if nothing else suggests eccentricity ran in the family.

Several things upset her about having the Olympic Games in her capital city in 1928. She wasn't sure about women taking part, for instance. But then nor were quite a few people. The Pope and Pierre de Coubertin, whose idea the Games had been, worried that women running around and getting sweaty and straining themselves would go away unable to have children. Not having children has always been a worry for the Vatican.

But worse than that, Queen Wil reckoned the Games were a demonstration of paganism. She never said as much in speeches but she did and she clearly didn't think much of the honor foisted on her land because she refused to attend the opening ceremony.

What makes the story odder is that the Queen seems to have known nothing about the Olympics being in Amsterdam. Not officially, anyway. She must have noticed the odd mention in the papers but nobody thought to ask if she was free that day. When finally someone consulted her, she sniffed that she'd arranged to go to Norway. Had friends there, no doubt. She sent her consort, Hendrik, to the Olympics instead and Wilhelmina became the first head of state to miss the opening ceremony. That meant she didn't see the Olympic torch being lit in the stadium, the first time it was done. She didn't see the flame being run through the streets, either, but that was more because it wasn't done until another difficult leader—although in a different way, of course—thought to do it in Berlin.

As it turned out, Pierre de Coubertin wasn't there either. Because he was ill. Nor was the Pope, because Popes don't usually go. So they couldn't decide for themselves whether the women's events were unladylike. Holland had added the 100-meter, 800-meter, 4 x 100-meter relay, high jump, discus and gymnastics for them.

In fact several women collapsed before or after the finish in the 800-meter, which Philip Noel-Baker, the head of the British contingent, agreed "was not a pleasant sight." Other officials rounded on him in a we-told-you-so way because Britain had campaigned for the women to take part. It was "a frightful episode," he said in his toff-like way, before sniffing that "the trouble was that the competitors had not been properly trained."

I don't know how long Wilhelmina stayed in Norway or even if, in the end, she actually went. Either she hurried back from the fjords or she had a change of mind because one day she startled all involved by announcing she wished to see the water polo.

You don't get dirty playing water polo but that doesn't make it a clean sport. Not for nothing do the judges now have cameras under the water to see who's trying to sink whom.

"Knowing something of how water polo was too often played," Noel-Baker said, "I approached the pool with trepidation and gave them a lecture which the Commissioner had ordained. During the first session in the water, the referee penalized and warned several members of the British team; and the crowd—the arena was packed—began to groan."

Noel-Baker barged into the team's area as the players stood dripping during the first pause. What did they think they were doing? The Queen was there, for heaven's sake. The pride of the Union Jack was at stake. They were to kindly start behaving themselves.

They did behave themselves and they won their heat. Then they met the Germans and Noel-Baker gave his men another stiff warning. But the Germans were either better or less scrupulous. Whichever it was, they sank the British and won the gold medal.

Noel-Baker thought all his life he'd done just the right thing in urging Britain not to cheat. But not everyone agreed. Years later he was at an Olympic party at 10 Downing Street, the prime minister's

The Olympics' 50 Craziest Stories

~

home. He was sipping and nattering when a broad-shouldered man pushed his way towards him.

"Remember me?", he asked bluntly.

Noel-Baker hesitated, trying to place the face.

"You may not know who I am," the giant said, "but I know who you are. You're the chap who lost us the gold medal in Amsterdam!"

Only he may not have said "the chap."

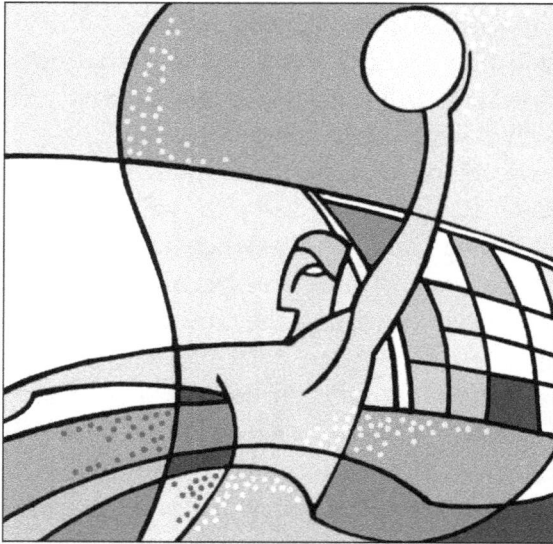

Les Woodland

2

How To Be Kind To Ducks

It is sometimes said that Australians aren't subtle. Bang your glass in a backlands bar, it's said, and you get to fight any sheep-shearer who fancies his chance. Restaurant waiters serve tea on a tray and shout "If you don't take sugar, don't stir it."

But there are exceptions. Henry Pearce was an exception, a gentle man who all but apologized to the frogs he disturbed as he made his way up the Olympic rowing course in Amsterdam that year. He would be famous enough for being the first singles sculler to win Olympic gold medals back-to-back. Which, when you think of the way rowers sit in their boats, isn't a bad way to put it. But what made his name across the world was his kindness to ducks.

Aussie Hal was known as Bobby. It seemed a good idea to name him after his father, who was also a champion rower, but having two Henrys became complicated and Henry the Second became Bobby the First.

The family may have been useless at names but it had good genes: Henry the First, who was actually the true Henry the Second because his own father had also been Henry—are you following this?—rowed but lost in the world championship finals of 1911 and 1913. Bobby's aunt was state swimming champion, an uncle made a national name at rugby, a cousin also rowed in the Olympics and another played rugby for Australia.

Bobby stood 1 meter 88 (6'2") and weighed 95 kilograms (209 pounds). That's a lot now but for 1928 it was colossal. It may have been all the food in his father's fish business. It was enough, anyway, for Bobby to be not only the sole Australian rower in the 1928 Olympics—held on the other side of the world, remember, when ships were the normal way to travel—but the man to carry the Oz flag at the opening ceremony.

The rowing was held on the Stoten canal, one of Amsterdam's many waterways. Pearce splashed off in the quarterfinal and soon led. Behind him he could see his French rival but in front of him, but when he chanced to look over his shoulder, he saw duck and a fleet of ducklings—at right angles to Olympic glory.

Rather than scatter them, Pearce stopped rowing and waited for them to pass. The Frenchman, called Saurin, who to be fair may never have seen the ducks, did no such thing. He stormed on by. (In case this is distressing you, no animals were hurt in the telling of this story.) Pearce then restarted rowing, passed Saurin and won by 20 lengths, setting a course record. The Queen didn't see him but saving the ducks made Pearce a favorite with the children of Holland.

As if this story weren't odd enough, it's worth recalling that Australia sent Pearce to Europe with plenty of time to recover, to train and to row other races. The one that appealed to him was the Diamond Sculls at Henley. It's probably stuffy even now but back then it was stifling. One rule, for instance, banned tradesmen. Men in blazers and straw boaters snorted when they heard this Australian was a a carpenter. They wouldn't let this colossus of the colonies start. Being a carpenter offended their idea of amateurism. This barred anyone who was "by trade or employment for wages a mechanic, artisan or laborer."

But a man who stops for ducks deserved better, and he got it. Two years later, Henley had to back down. The brothers who ran the Dewar's whisky empire approached Pearce after he won the Empire Games single sculls in Ontario in 1930. Would he be their sales representative there? Pearce said he would. That meant he was no longer a carpenter, which is just what the Dewar brothers had in mind. They entered him for Henley again and rightly described him as a salesman. The boat-and-boater brigade accepted him. And Pearce won the race easily.

What became of him? Well, he became a professional rower, doubtless not a crowded profession. And then in 1939 he took up professional wrestling. He joined the Canadian navy when war started—apt for a man who made his name on the water—became a Canadian in 1972 and died of a heart attack four years later.

What became of the ducks, I have no idea. They may even not have noticed.

16   *Les Woodland*

• • •

Canoeing organizers in the austerity London Games of 1948 had to provide boats in a hurry and for not much money. They melted surplus windows from wartime fighters and bombers and then "We found a man at Chertsey with what we considered an average-shape bottom and sat him naked in a box of plaster of Paris, to make a mold. We boiled water in a metal dustbin lid over a Primus stove and softened a piece of Perspex in that. We quickly put it on the mold and sat our stooge on that, ignoring his yells and putting someone on his shoulders to apply pressure."

A problem arose when some teams turned up with their own, crooked canoes. They'd found that putting a bend in the boat corrected its tendency to go in one direction more than the other. The Olympic report says: "Naturally, this gives a man in a crooked canoe an advantage over an opponent who must steer and drive, and protests were registered with the ICF some days before the competition. These were rejected on the ground that this form of construction did not violate the existing building rule, since a curved keel is not a rudder in the accepted sense of the word. It was agreed, however, that such a development was undesirable."

• • •

Rowers come on the large size, coxes on the small. They all go to the podium together. The British pair in the coxed pairs at Barcelona in 1992 were steered by a little chap called Garry Herbert. The race was still in doubt when he shouted "Do you want to make a little bit of magic?" to the brothers Greg and Jonny Searle in the boat ahead of him. They did, he called a faster pace, and they won. The top of Cox's head came barely higher than the brothers' shoulders. And when the anthem played, his face crumpled and, in Gordon Thompson's words: "He stood in front of the giant brothers, crying his eyes out, in the manner of a first-former who has just had his dinner money taken by the school bullies."

Far from losing his small cash, Herbert now charges up to £5,000 for dinner speeches.

The Olympics' 50 Craziest Stories   17

*

• • •

Russia's Vyacheslav Ivanov was so thrilled at winning a gold medal in Melbourne that he jumped for joy—and dropped his medal in the water. He plunged in to find it but it was never seen again.

• • •

Who watches most Olympics on tv?

Japan	30 hours 29 minutes
Indonesia	26 hours 37 minutes
Finland	24 hours 12 minutes
Australia	23 hours 42 minutes
Iceland	22 hours 12 minutes
Argentina	20 hours 31 minutes
Sweden	19 hours 34 minutes
Bosnia-Herzegovina	18 hours 36 minutes
Denmark	18 hours 7 minutes
Greece	17 hours 33 minutes

Source: Athens 2004

Les Woodland

Five Things You Didn't Know You Didn't Know...About TV

1. More than 203 million Americans watched the Athens Games in 2004.

2. China broadcast 53 hours of Athens, each watched by an average of 85 million.

3. The first closed-circuit pictures were to 25 public buildings in Berlin in 1936. More than 160,000 watched.

4. True broadcasting happened for the first time in London in 1948. Reception was limited to 80 kilometers of London, although the Channel Islands saw good pictures when the weather changed.

5. The American network, NBC, paid $545 million for rights to the 2002 winter Games.

3

How Not To Be An Officer And A Gentleman

The rule about tradesmen not being amateurs wasn't new. Edward Battel and his colleague Frank Keeping were servants at the British embassy in Athens in 1896 when, hearing about the new Olympics, they entered for the bike races. There was no objection from the organizers—anyone was free to take part—but there was a great fuss from the British.

Until then Britain had taken little notice of the games. "Sport", in Britain, still meant hunting and shooting. But there were limits, by golly, and a nation that ruled half the earth wasn't about to let two bearers of drinks trays to represent it. Searching the rule books, they found this business about amateurism. It's true the servants had never been paid to compete and nor had they accepted money in prizes. But the very fact that they had a job showed they needed money, that they didn't have a private income, and therefore that they might be *tempted* to take money.

Battel and Keeping were ruled out.

That made the British figures of fun and the world laughed. The Empire retreated with a hurrumph and let them compete. You'd think news of the Empire's retreat would have reached the stuffy types at Henley but they didn't drop their objection to the common man until 1937.

Battel rode the road race and came third, bruised and bleeding after crashing on the rutted roads from Athens to Marathon and back. Keeping rode the 12-hour race on the track, where he finished with 899 laps to the 900 of Austria's Adolf Schmal. The race started at 5 AM with just six riders, four of them Greek, and few people turned out to watch because, say reports, "it was a monotonous sight."

The spectacle they missed was of Keeping and Schmal growing more and more wretched until both could barely continue. Richard D. Mandell, in *The First Modern Olympics*, says: "They were squalid from excreta and delirious from fatigue… their legs swollen gruesomely… both could be heard weeping."

Even slower to join the modern world was the horse community. Gehnäll Persson—an august-looking, long-faced man known as Gene—was riding in the London Olympics when someone spotted he had the wrong hat. Not too serious, you'd have thought, except that Persson was wearing a sergeant's hat and the dressage was open only to commissioned officers. The governing body, the FEI, wanted only officers and gentlemen to take part. Not even the wives of gentlemen could compete.

The problem was that, lowly ranker or not, Persson won the dressage for Sweden along with his colleagues Major Henri Saint Cyr and Captain Gustaf Boltenstern. And they were just getting their medals when Georges Hector, the 80-year-old Frenchman at the head of the world equestrian federation, called the ceremony to a halt. More than 20 years as the FEI's secretary-general hadn't passed without learning to spot a man in a sergeant's hat.

It wasn't that Sweden hadn't known the rules. They'd known a good year and had talked about them at length. Persson was too good to leave out of the team, though, and so the Swedes had given him a temporary promotion to second-lieutenant. After the Games he'd be demoted to sergeant again and return to the K4 Norland Dragoons. Well, the most devious plans can fall on the most minor of points and Sweden fell at the first hurdle—if that's not a mixed metaphor for a sport which involves making a horse walk sideways—because it hadn't found him an officer's cap. Persson had gone to the podium as a sergeant. Sadly for him, Hectoring Hector was a uniform enthusiast and not only Persson's medal but those of the entire team were awarded and then taken away. It took a year to do it but do it Hector did it.

What made the episode still more farcical is that Hector's decision moved his fellow Frenchmen from second to first, which may not have been his aim but didn't go unnoticed. The Games report says tactfully that "unfortunately the Swedish team was later disqualified as one of their members was not qualified to compete." The sport was ridiculed and the rules changed for the Helsinki Games in 1952. Not only non-rankers could take part but women as well.

Happily, Officer Persson returned in 1952 and 1956 and won the event he had been denied in 1948. He died in July 1976.

You think that was all? Jack Kelly, a world-class rower who happened to be the father of Princess Grace of Monaco, couldn't row at Henley because he'd been a bricklayer.

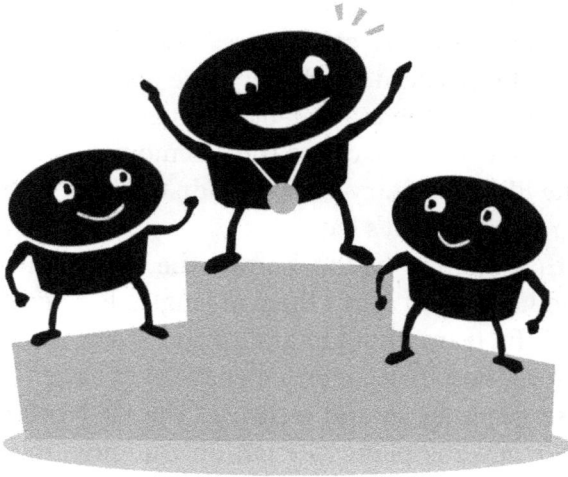

Les Woodland

Five Olympic Mascots You Wish You'd Forget

If ever medals were given to the Olympics rather than by them, there should be a gold for contributions to the fluffy toy industry. And disqualification by the judges of good taste.

They feel like they've been around for ever, those irritating dolls and sometimes just odd shapes that peer from drinks bottles, margarine packets and anything ever made by anyone who has stumped up money to be called an Official Supplier. They have spread from the Olympics into hitherto saner sports, so that many can't begin until an enormous duck has waddled across the grass with its wings flapping.

Things are bad enough when there's just one. Sometimes both teams bring one. In one entertaining moment, rival dress-ups disputed who was to have best place in front of the stands during the warm-up and the crowd was entertained instead to a fight between a huge panda and a frog. Or was it a cuddly bear and a pig?

In fact they've been around only since the Munich Games of 1972. So how can you forget, however hard you try…

1. *Waldi the German dachshund.* Waldi was the Munich mascot. The normally logical Germans realized that sausage dogs are not only what everyone associates with Germany (although they didn't think to point that out) but that they are resistant, tenacious and agile. This would be all very well if for some reason the Germans hadn't then lost their presence of

mind and given Waldi blue, orange, yellow and green stripes. He must have looked wonderful on LSD, but by then there were drug tests and nobody found out.

2. *Izzy the, er, whatever it was.* Atlanta in 1996 made many unforgettable contributions to Olympic history, not least transport chaos and a wonky computer. The art department was obviously keen to emphasize the role of the microchip in Atlanta society because it said from the start that Izzy was designed by a computer. In the context, "designed" was an unusual word. Izzy looked as though the computer had been turned on and off a few times while it was working. He had a blue face and, embarrassingly for a Southern city, eyes and lips made up in thick white like a vaudeville minstrel. The rest of him, in blue, red and yellow, looked like a soggy Superman, but with a multicolored stumpy tale.

The marketing people didn't know what to make of him because they called him Izzy. Short for "What is it?"

3. *Syd, Olly and Millie.* There's a lot of space in Australia so Melbourne chose not one but three mascots for 2000. Bad taste didn't desert them. Syd, Olly and Millie are the sort of names you find in backstreet car-repair shops. In fact, said the sales people, Syd stood for Sydney, Olly for a kookaburra (maybe Kookie sounded too, er, kookie) and Millie recognized that the Games were starting a millennium. They were supposed to have been a platypus, some sort of duck and possibly a bright yellow hedgehog. All, we were told, were native Australian species. Maybe now they're wondering why they didn't just pick a kangaroo instead.

4. *Athenà and Pèvos.* No, it's no use asking me what they were. Nobody else knew, either. There probably isn't a name for a creature with a cone-shaped body, legs like frogs' flippers and a disarmingly vacant expression on a face held high by a long and fat neck. They were the choice of Athens in 2004. Only the fact that nobody else understood either keeps them from the top

of the forgettable list. You want to know the official explanation? It was that Phèvos, in an orange patterned dress of the sort your mother used to wear, was the brother of Athenà, who wears a sky-blue nightdress. One was the god of light and music and the other the goddess of wisdom. A quality that deserted Greece in 2004.

5. *Sam the Eagle.* If the Australians missed a chance to have a kangaroo, you'd expect Americans to overlook Uncle Sam. But, no, there he was for Los Angeles in 1984, a gaudy tribute to the power of primary colors. Uncle Sam on the posters looks a commanding, authoritative figure. And the eagle that is America's national symbol is a distinguished bird at the top of the tree. It took the skill of Walt Disney to change all that. The yellow-faced eagle looked like a bath tub duck and Uncle Sam just looked ridiculous, every inch fit for Disneyland. He wore a concave, red-striped top hat and a bright red shirt with a floppy red and white bow tie. But nothing beneath the waist. Which was a dreadful oversight for Disney.

4

How To Be A Champion And Not Know It

Margaret Ives Abbott's story fascinates—but not only because she became an Olympic champion without knowing.

Marda, as her family called her, was a well-bred young lady from a fortunate background. She lived with her mother, Mary, in Chicago, where they had moved from India. Margaret was born in Calcutta in 1876. She and her mother joined the Chicago Golf Club and learned the art of putting and driving from one of the country's best amateurs, Charles Blair MacDonald.

They were socialites, searchers for social status, and their apartment in Charlevoix on the swanky north side of Chicago was a site of constant parties and soirées. But unalloyed pleasure does nothing for a girl and in 1899 the pair left for Paris, where Marda was to study art under Dégas and Rodin, and the two visited the Paris Exhibition before setting off on a Grand Tour of Europe. At some time Mary planned to write a novel.

In Paris they heard of a good golf match going on. Marda was the best woman player in Illinois and her mother wasn't much worse. So they joined in. The Paris Games, the second after Athens, were neither well organized nor well publicized. Marda and Mary weren't alone in not knowing where they were. Many of the track and field athletes had no idea either. Michel Théato of Luxembourg found out only 12 years later that he had won the marathon (amid, it must be said, claims that he had taken short cuts through the back streets of Paris). When France tried to find all its Olympic representatives, they confused an old man on his doorstep by telling him he had been one of them. He denied it.

The Olympic Games, edited by Lord Killanin and John Rodda, recounts: "In about 1965, the French Olympic Committee discovered that a certain Vasserot, ranked second in the speed cycling event, was still alive. When questioned, the veteran vaguely remembered he had raced in 1900 on the track at Vincennes. No one had told him at the time that he had taken part in the Olympic Games. He died in 1968 as a 'silver medalist.'"

The book put "silver medallist" in quotes because the records were as shaky as the old boy's memory. The first three in the sprint had been two Frenchmen and an American called John Henry Lake. Vasserot, it appeared, had been beaten by Lake in the semifinal and hadn't been a medalist at all.

The golf, to get back to the story, was nine holes rather than 18. Many of the 11 women taking part misunderstood what they were up to and wore tight skirts and high heels. Marda finished first after shooting 47. Her mother came seventh with 65 and she and Mary are the only mother and daughter in the Olympics to have competed in the same competition. Two further Americans, Polly Whittier and Hugar Pratt, came second and third. Women had only just been allowed at the Games, restricted to golf, tennis and croquet. Although it seems that even that was decided retrospectively because Paris forced a decision by including women's competitions against the will of the international Games committee.

Marda never realized what she'd won because, said Killanin and Rodda's book, the Games "comprised an unbelievable muddle of sports, some officially recognized, some not recognized, world amateur championships and professional championships, scattered over the four corners of the capital. There was constant confusion. The public couldn't make head or tail of the events, nor could the reporters. Even today it is difficult to sort out the wheat from the chaff among the prizewinners."

Such is the confusion that the best bet now is that Marda and Charles Sands, who won the men's event, actually went to play tennis. There seems evidence that it was more an Olympic sport than golf. In that case, Marda knew she was at the Olympic Games. Word probably spread that there was a golf game to be played and Marda and her mother entered. The fact that none of the top players were there, and that many in the women's match wore fashion clothes, backs a theory that golf had been just relaxation for whoever wanted to take part and was only later promoted to an Olympic competition. That happened to cricket, an even more unlikely sport for the French to include.

Well, Marda may not have won a medal but she found a husband. She married Finley Dunne, an American humorist and fellow socialite who'd gone to France to see the Exhibition and the Games that formed a minor part of them. Finley died in 1936 and Marda in 1955, neither ever realizing she was an Olympic champion. It took even longer than that to establish that golf had indeed been part of the Paris Olympics.

Les Woodland

5

How Not To Organize
An Olympics (1)

Things couldn't have been more chaotic in Paris. And it wasn't just the golf. The point to remember is that the Olympics weren't yet The Olympic Games. Nobody knew if they'd catch on and still fewer thought them important. The King of Greece did because, after the revival in 1896, he insisted his country had exclusive rights to run them. Americans agreed. And when de Coubertin hesitated, the King told him to agree or to resign.

Well, de Coubertin hadn't got that far without knowing a ruse or two. He pretended not to understand. And he skipped off and gave the Games to his own country's capital.

The King got over his upset but the body that ran French athletics, the USFSA, never did. It was jealous and, with some foresight, worried that the Olympics would grow bigger than it was. So whatever de Coubertin proposed, the USFSA objected—even though he was its secretary-general.

De Coubertin wanted the USFSA to run the Games for him. The USFSA, because that's the way it was inclined, said it wouldn't. So de Coubertin, finding nobody else, tacked his Games on to the Universal Exhibition to be held in Paris. Its head man, Alfred Picart, thought sport was an absurd and pointless activity. So when de Coubertin planned to build temples and statues and reproductions of Roman baths, he dropped the plan in a drawer and never looked at it again.

Grudgingly, he accepted to accommodate "exhibitions of physical exercise and sports" provided they were at unpopular venues and incorporated with whatever else was going on there. So athletics became part of the exhibition of savings banks, fencing was filed under cutlery and rowing, almost aptly, was included with exhibitions of lifesaving.

The rowing never did go off well, by the way. Far from the image of the gentle, duck-loving Bobby Pearce, those who took part were "coarse fellows, noisy, rowdy, who under the name of boatmen, spread terror among the peaceful riverside inhabitants." The Dutch pair, lacking a cox because their original choice was too heavy, are said to have dragged a seven-year-old boy off the street.

De Coubertin agreed to "exhibitions" but planned international competitions for the élite. The USFSA said it wanted nothing to do with a private sports meeting that formed part of a commercial exhibition and it pulled out. Paris appointed a committee of titled and military folk to take over but that was just as disastrous and a year before the Games opened they'd resigned and there was nobody in charge at all.

Nor was anybody inclined to join in if it entailed building Roman baths and setting the Games in the park of a château at Courbevoie. De Coubertin doubtless sobbed and went back to Plan A—the simplest Games possible.

The exhibition people were no more inclined to help and so the different sports were scattered around the city with no opening or closing ceremony—those were to come later—and no coherence. At times the Games descended into farce, as when trees on the sports ground at Croix-Catelan got in the way of the hammer and discus. Rudolf Bauer of Hungary avoided the trees but three times sent the discus into the crowd.

Sometimes the timetable and travel were so chaotic that competitors never reached their events or, because they were held on Sunday, refused to take part. When they did take part, runners found their hurdles were made from broken telephone poles. The swimming—including an obstacle race—was held in the Seine along with the city's trash and a strong current.

Professionals took part in the fencing for a prize of 3,000 francs. And just now and then events entered the absurd, with fire-fighting, pigeon-shooting, ballooning and long-jump for horses. And this all

Les Woodland

lasted five months, from May to October, the length of the Exhibition. There were more participants than spectators.

It was the Olympic Games, but perhaps not as we know it.

6

How To…Hang On—Did I Read That Right?

Did they really shoot live pigeons in the Paris Olympics? Well, yes, they certainly did. The Olympics movement is embarrassed by it and doesn't include the results in its records. But it was there and it was won by Léon de Lunden of Belgium, who split his prize of 20,000 francs with the next three.

The rules were remarkably simple: birds would fly in the sky one by one and the winner was whoever shot down most. Around 300 lay bloody and lifeless or painfully flapping their broken wings on the ground by the time the day was over, de Lunden having accounted for 21. It was too much even in the more callous atmosphere of the time. The American writer, Andrew Strunk, said: "Maimed birds were writhing on the ground, blood and feathers were swirling in the air and women with parasols were weeping in the chairs set up nearby."

Shooters were eliminated once they'd missed two birds. Maurice Faure of France came second with 20 dead birds on his conscience and Donald MacKintosh, a Scotsman competing for Australia, and Crittenden Robinson of the USA, tied in third with 18.

Why doesn't the Olympic movement record the results? Well, embarrassment could be one reason. In fact, it insists the shooting wasn't formally a Games event, although it was certainly held during the Olympics.

Live birds were replaced by clay pigeons for the next Games, at St. Louis in 1904. But, if shooting of pigeons continued—albeit of artificial ones—does that not suggest that the slaughter of June 27, 1900, was perhaps more official than the Games cared then to admit? It wasn't the shooting to which it objected, only the target.

Les Woodland

• • •

Life may have grown safer for the pigeons of Paris but the 1924 Olympics in the city weren't more secure for the shooters. The American, Sid Hinds, scored a perfect 50 to win the free-rifle competition. Fair enough: lots of people win gold medals. Yes, but not after being shot first by one of his rivals. A Belgian competitor accidentally dropped his rifle; it went off and shot Hinds in the foot. Hinds went on to be a general in the American army and fought his way across the Rhine to cut off the German advance in the Ardennes. It was a great deal safer than the Olympic Games.

ॐ

7

How To Win Hands Down

George Seymour Lyon had tried baseball, tennis and cricket. And he'd been quite good at them. He even held the Canadian record for pole-vaulting. What he'd never tried was golf. So when someone challenged him, he had a go. He was 38, a bit old to perfect new tricks, and he swiped his a golf club like a baseball bat in what one reporter called a coalheaver's swing and a New York critic said was like "using a scythe to cut wheat."

But Lyon loved the game, troubled little about the criticism because he kept winning matches. At 39 he won the Canadian amateur championship—winning again in 1900 and 1903. And eight years after he first picked up a club he headed down from Toronto to play at the Olympics in St. Louis. He bounded round the course, singing, cracking jokes and pulling off handstands. He won one round by 11 holes with nine to play. He then won the whole competition and will be remembered as the only Olympic champion to have walked to the prize ceremony on his hands. He collected a silver trophy worth $1,500.

The 1908 Games in London wanted to give him a gold medal before he'd even played. He was the only player to show up. British golfers were in a huff over a row with the organizers and stayed away. Other nations, seeing that, also stayed at home. It left Lyon the only man there—and in a quandary because it's not every day a man wins an Olympic gold and even less often that he gets it for nothing. But his conscience got the better of him and he declined. The medal was never awarded.

Lyon went home and won Canadian titles in 1905, 1906, 1907 and 1912. He played senior competitions after the first world war and won every year but three from 1918 to 1930. He'd have won in 1929 had he not dropped out before the final to go to his son's wedding. He died in Toronto in 1938. By then golf had been dropped from the Olympics for 34 years.

Not that it was alone in disappearing or that Lyon was the only person to turn up and find nobody else there. There were so many sailing races in 1920 that seven—half the total—had only one boat. It's easy to forget that the Olympic movement for many years had to persuade people to take part. Now it's an honor but for decades there was little interest in sitting in a ship heading slowly for the other side of the world.

The solution for the International Olympic Committee was to include as many sports as it could, especially what now seem arcane or games played by only a few countries. Erich Kamper, a Games historian, says: "In this way it was hoped to increase recognition and popularity for sports of less than worldwide appeal. Cricket, croquet, golf, lacrosse, roque (a form of croquet played on a court with a hard raised edge used as a cushion in bank shots) and rugby football were among such sports. They did not become permanent because the organizers of the following Games would lose interest in them and look on their continuation as a needless burden."

Among the casualties were the long jump from a standing start (which an American called Ray Ewry won 10 times), the tug-of-war (in which the City of London police beat Stockholm police in 1908 thanks to their specialist shoes) and the underwater swimming.

This last was in the Seine in Paris in 1900—the only time it has been held—with a point for every second submerged and two points for every meter swum. The first two were French but the perils of swimming in one of Europe's filthiest rivers were the same for everyone.

Still more exciting was the swimming obstacle race that same year. The course, with the current and 200 meters long, required competitors to climb over a pole and swim under and clamber over boats.

Motor-boating vanished after its only appearance, in 1904, and curiosities such as throwing the javelin, discus and shot with both hands appeared and vanished four years later. And an event called the 100-meter freestyle "for sailors" didn't return after 1896.

The Olympics' 50 Craziest Stories   35

Five Olympians Wearing Rings

To take part is better than to win. Is that what the sage said? Something like that. For many athletes, merely getting to the Games is the greatest moment of their lives. One which has marked them. Literally.

1. The British cyclist Chris Boardman has the Olympic rings tattooed on his shoulder.

2. Miguel Rodriguez of Honduras had the Olympic rings and the three Korean symbols for "taekwondo" tattooed inside his right arm.

3. Ned Gerard, who took part in the shooting for the Virgin Islands, had the Olympic rings tattooed on his wrist.

4. Daniel Bell, a swimmer from New Zealand, had the rings cut into his hair.

5. The canoeist Tomasz Wylenzek of Germany has both the rings and "Athens 2004" tattooed on his right shoulder.

8

How Not To Organize
An Olympics (2)

The Paris Olympics may have been chaotic. But they were nothing compared to the next Games, in St. Louis. Which other Olympics has offered "native-friendly" competitions such as tree-climbing? Or shot-putting by pygmies?

"I was not only present at a sporting contest but also at a fair where there were sports, where there was cheating, where monsters were exhibited for a joke," wrote de Coubertin's man on the spot. The competitions pitted African pygmies, Patagonians, Filipinos, Turks, Sioux Indians and other colored races against each other and drew more people than actual Olympics. "With a gigantic effort," says one report, "a pygmy dispatched the regulation weight three meters."

A local newspaper reported: "The unique spectacle of men deliberately throwing stones at one another will be one of the features of the athletic meet…in which all of the savage tribes now at the World's Fair will compete." Other events included rope-climbing by Filipinos and a mud-throwing contest between pygmies.

Among Filipino visitors were 100 headhunters from northern Luzon, who were said to eat dogs and rumored to snare local pets to satisfy their hunger. Other tribes were displayed eating elephant and monkey and worms and grasshoppers. The aim was to demonstrate the superiority of Anglo-Saxons over supposed primitives. "Savages" were displayed in need of the civilizing presence of the white man, specifically of American white men.

The official report of the Games regretted the standard of the men's running ("very poor"), javelin ("another disappointment"), archery ("another disappointment"), and weight-tossing abilities ("the savages did not take kindly at all to the 56 pound weight"). It asked in a saddened but firm tone: "Lecturers and authors will in the future please omit all reference to the natural athletic ability of the savage, unless they can substantiate their alleged feats."

The Games were run with an exhibition celebrating America's buying of Louisiana from France, the theme of the World's Fair. Judy Garland's family went there in "Meet Me in St. Louis". There were the ordinary industrial and scientific exhibits, plus the world's largest organ, Lincoln's boyhood cabin, newly developed food such as peanut butter—and a human zoo.

The Olympics had originally been given to Chicago. But St. Louis had put a lot into its show and it didn't want Chicago drawing customers to another part of the country. If Chicago didn't back down, the Missourians would organize a sports event larger than the Olympics could ever be. Thereby disgracing it. De Coubertin backed down. He stayed away, too, predicting that "the Olympiad would match the mediocrity of the town."

Natives employed as actors at the show were enrolled by William J. McGee, an anthropologist, and by a showy sports promoter called James E. Sullivan, a smiling man with a thick mustache. Their sports events would have the "scientific" goal of measuring "savages" against "civilized men". Their problem was that these backward, grinning savages were brighter than they thought. They were taking part because they were being paid. Some lived not on remote islands but in the American Midwest. And while they were happy shimmying up trees or acting out supposed everyday scene from native life, they did it because they were being paid. And they expected to be paid again.

By then the native games had been advertised and spectators sought. This was no time to back down. McGee and Sullivan were forced to cancel their water polo matches but they did find enough recruits in the human zoo for everything else.

Things didn't start well. The first day included shot put, high jump, long jump and running a mile. The competitors spoke so many languages that neither the rules nor the technique could be passed on adequately. Three men were persuaded to throw a 56 pound weight but then they lost interest and wandered off rather than hold a second heat. Many of the runners had never heard of, still less heard,

Les Woodland

a starting pistol and didn't know what to do. Nor did things improve with the "savage-friendly" tree-climbing, fighting demonstrations and mud-throwing on the second day. McGee had assumed that all savages could at least throw a spear and was horrified to find that most had little idea what to do with a javelin.

He and Sullivan were pleased to note, though, that savages showed their inferiority by not mastering tennis. Four years later, when Sullivan was secretary of the US Olympic Committee, the Games were fully opened to women. He refused to let American women take part.

His anthropological games attracted so much attention not just for their oddity and shamefulness but because the main Games were so lackluster. They were the first outside Europe—the Olympic idea was still establishing itself—and few overseas athletes made the trip. Most events had only Americans taking part. Those back home who read what had happened decided they'd made the right choice: the swimming, for instance, was held on an irregular lake and the times, said Gaston Meyer, founder of the French Athletic Club, were "hardly worthy of beach swimmers today."

The 1904 Games were, though, the first with gold, silver and bronze medals. Boxing appeared for the first time—but only Americans took part.

There'd have been more Americans at the next Games, in London in 1908, had Sullivan agreed to send any women. Both he and the Olympics had moved on: Sullivan to be head of the American Olympic committee and the Games to formally include women. That wasn't something Sullivan subscribed to and women were simply left at home.

Sullivan did nothing but complain when he got to London. He came close to an official protest a day for the length of the Games. It got him into all the scandal papers and it secured his place in American sports officialdom but it made him no friends internationally. His team did well, he said, but only despite the British. He named a string of officials, said their behavior was "outrageous not only to Americans, but contrary to their own rules, and if these men continue to dictate affairs, England will become athletically degenerate."

"Degenerate"… from the man who organized mud-throwing, tree-climbing and events for pygmies.

The Olympics' 50 Craziest Stories

∞

9

How To Turn Wood To Gold

There are several claimants to the title of most improbable Olympian but few can beat George Eyser. For in 1904 gymnastics he won the parallel bars, long horse vault and rope climbing, came second in the pommel horse and a competition based on four events, and third on the horizontal bar.

That he won six medals all in one day and in one sport was astonishing enough; that he did it in gymnastics is as odd as it gets. Because he is the only Olympic medal-winner to have had a wooden leg. Which, if it hindered him nowhere else, couldn't have helped in the rope-climbing.

Eyser was born in Germany, where he was known as Georg Eÿser. He moved to America at 14 when his parents emigrated. Quite when and how a train ran over his left leg has escaped history but it seems to have been with just one leg that he became an American citizen in 1894. And it was with one healthy leg and a wooden one that he took up gymnastics. The sport was less of a mystery to him than to others because it had started in Germany, as *turnverein*, only a few decades earlier. By then he lived in St. Louis—unmarried and renting a single room—so there seemed no point in not entering the Olympics when it was held in town, especially since his sports club was sending a team.

The mystery is not only how he became so good but what happened to him afterwards. Biographers have repeatedly come back empty-handed from searches of public records, both in St. Louis and nationally. By 1920 he had left St. Louis but nobody knows for where. It appears he had sisters but still nobody knows when he died, where he was buried or even what happened to his medals. Was he, for instance,

a victim of the flu epidemic which swept the world and killed more people than the first world war? Did he die an old man, unknown to his neighbors but armed by his memories?

Nobody knows.

10

How To Turn Gold To Ashes

Fred Lorz knew a good laugh when it came his way. And a chuckle was what he needed because he worked all day in New York as a bricklayer and then ran for hours at night. That training brought him fourth place in the Boston marathon and so he decided to enter the Olympics.

He was running the marathon at St. Louis, and he pretty soon grew tired of the heat—which forced all but 14 of the 32 starters to quit—and of the dust kicked up by cars and horses that cleared the dirt road. He had run nine miles, about a third of the course, when his manager offered to drive him to the finish. They set off but their car broke down after 11 miles and Lorz continued on foot, leaving his boss to peer at the engine. Despite being driven so far, Lorz must have taken his time because he got in only just before those who had run all the way. Finish-line officials thought he had won the race. In fact he had merely gone to collect his clothes.

Fred saw the joke and began to go through with the medal ceremony. His home crowd cheered loudly and the president's daughter, Alice Roosevelt, put a laurel wreath on his head. Only then did the judges realize the truth. They banned him first for life and then, when other runners said it was clear he hadn't tried to trick them because they'd seen him waving from the car, for a year. He didn't give up running, though, and in 1905 he won the Boston marathon. And he carried on running it until 1908. He died of pneumonia six years later.

The actual winner, Tom Hicks, almost died on the finish line. He and Lorz knew each other because Hicks had come second in the 1904 Boston race, two places ahead of Lorz. That prompted him, too, to go to St. Louis.

Hicks lived in Cambridge, Massachusetts, where he worked in a brass foundry. He had been born in England but at some point his

Les Woodland

parents had emigrated to Boston. There, he met a man called Charles J. P. Lucas who taught him about running.

Lucas was one of those shady, self-aggrandizing men who have always hung about at sports events. He was referred to as Hicks' "handler". One of his claims was that he had qualified from the medical school at Harvard University, on Boston's outskirts. That made him, by his own estimation, more or less a doctor. His own athletic prowess, however, went no further than winning stone-gathering competitions and potato races.

Hicks started the Olympic marathon under Lucas' gaze and led from the start. Then he slowed to a walk on a small hill after 19 miles. The New York Times reported: "Hicks was running with a mechanical exactness, slowly and with every motion of his body indicating by its regularity and apparent effort that he was suffering from fatigue."

Lucas was there with his medical skills. He said, in his account of the race, that he gave Hicks a milligram of strychnine mixed with two egg whites. Strychnine, in small doses, was sport's most popular stimulant before the advent of amphetamine.

Hicks was dehydrated and exhausted. The strychnine did him little good because he stumbled on for another mile and then stopped, gray-faced. Lucas was there again and gave him another milligram of strychnine, this time in brandy. Athletes believed that alcohol increased the effect of other drugs they were taking, and drink lessened their pain and tedium.

Another rise led to the stadium, where the race had started with five laps of the track, and Hicks made it without quite realizing what was going on. He was babbling deliriously. His cheers were subdued not by the crowd's shock but because spectators still thought Lorz had won. Hicks was helped across the line and then fell. He was carried off the track and taken to doctors. Eventually Lorz's ruse was discovered and the barely conscious Hicks was named the winner.

If the crowd had realized what had increased his distress, said the doping historian Daniel M. Rosen, it wouldn't have disapproved. "Back in those days, the use of performance-enhancing substances was not the awful thing it is today," he said. "Hicks was kind of a hero for doing everything he could to win. But he damn near killed himself in the process."

In fact, the final controversy wasn't that Hicks was drugged—but that others weren't drugged. Strychnine hadn't been available for everyone. Lucas encouraged that sympathy. "The marathon race, from a medical standpoint, demonstrated that drugs are of much benefit to athletes along the road, and that warm sponging is much better than cold sponging for an athlete in action," he trumpeted. "Hicks was far from being the best man physically in the race, for there were three men who should have defeated him…but they lacked proper care on the road."

The experience couldn't have done Hicks too much harm: he recovered, collected his medal a few days later, and lived until the end of 1963.

Les Woodland

Five Competitors Who Wish They Hadn't Done It

1. The Norwegian skier Odd-Bjoern flopped in the ski run at Vancouver in 2010. It cost him the gold medal. Asked why, he said in excellent English: "I skied the second lap and I *** up today. By the way, Tiger Woods is a really good man."

2. Snow boarding is a hip sport and, while nobody else may have heard of anyone taking part, the riders are gods to insiders. Enough that when the American Scotty Largo hung his medal on a ribbon long enough to take it to his fly, a female fan was anxious to get down and lick it. The pictures turned up, complete with Largo in a Team USA shirt, and America sent him home before he could do any more damage.

3. The British runner Daley Thompson was born for the seventies. He had the brashness, the lack of taste and, most important, the mustache. *The Times* of London called him "objectionable, charmless and rude." But Britain loved him—up to a point. That point was reached in Los Angeles in 1984 when he won a gold medal and ran round the stadium in a T-shirt reading "Is the world's 2nd greatest athlete gay?" It was taken as referring to Carl Lewis. But then what would you expect of a man whose ambition was "to give Princess Anne a baby"? Curiously, he was made an ambassador for the 2012 Games in London.

4. Spanish competitors in the men's and women's basketball teams for 2008 posed in the daily paper, *Marca*, pulling back their faces to look slit-eyed. That year's Games were in Beijing.

5. Hans-Gunnar Liljenwall, a Swedish pentathlete, fancied a drink at Mexico in 1968. Well, one or two drinks maybe. Certainly more than he should have had. Because the alcohol turned up in a drugs test after Sweden won the bronze medal and the team was disqualified. The pentathlon involves pistol shooting. Alcohol calms the nerves and steadies the aim. Which is why he was thrown out, the first positive in the Olympics.

Les Woodland

11

How Not To Run A Marathon

Lorz and Hicks are prime examples of how not to do it. But there are more. There is something about the marathon that brings out the wackiness in life.

As if those two eccentrics weren't enough in one race, there was also the Cuban postman, Andarin Carbajal. His full name was Félix de la Caridad Carbajal y Soto, but that was too long to get on an envelope and so friends called him Andarin. Why Andarin, when there is nothing in his name to prompt that? I have no idea.

Carbajal, a lean figure with a mustache as wide as his face, was a poor man who sometimes begged for money on the streets of Havana. His talent for running gave him an idea: he'd race round the streets and then ask for money. In that way he could collect enough to take a freight ship to New Orleans.

He was perhaps too naive to cope with the sharp-suits he met when he got there and he lost his remaining cash in dice games. He finally got to St. Louis by hitchhiking and hiding in freight trains.

He had nowhere to stay in St. Louis, having neither a sponsor nor the support of the Cuban athletics organization, but he made friends with the American weightlifters. They found him a place to sleep and food to eat.

The only clothes he had were those in which he'd arrived. That was how he went to the start. But they were out of the question in that heat and at the last moment one of the throwers, a New York policeman named Martin Sheridan, cut off Carbajal's pants at the knees.

He led from the start. But, like many taking part, he soon felt tired and hungry. He hadn't eaten for 40 hours. Spotting an orchard, he took a detour and helped himself to apples. They weren't as good as they might have been and a while later his stomach began to cramp.

Not knowing what to do, he lay down to sleep it off. By the time he felt better, so many runners had dropped out that he could carry on and come fourth.

Competing, too, were Len Tau—short for Len Taunyane—and his friend, Jan Mashiani. Jan, too, had changed his name for the race, calling himself Yamasani. They were the first two black Africans in the Games, although they'd come to St. Louis to take part in a Boer War exhibit at the World's Fair. There they were described as Tswana tribesmen and obliged the crowd by acting out tribal behavior to the crowd. In reality they were students from the Orange Free State.

Tau came ninth and Mashiani twelfth. Tau felt he might have done better had he not been chased a mile in the wrong direction by fierce dogs.

History so often repeats itself. Not only did Pietri Dorando also collapse in the marathon, this time in 1908, but he also competed under a different name. Runner number 19 was a pastry cook from the Isle of Capri, listed in the program as Pietri Dorando. The crowd knew no difference because the Italian runner was unknown. Only his mother knew she had called him Dorando Pietri. The program editor inadvertently reversed his names and it's as Pietri Dorando that he has gone into history.

Why? Because on July 24, 1908, he finally made up a four-minute gap on the South African, Charles Hefferon, and he ran into the stadium in his red shorts and white vest, a handkerchief round his head. There, confused, exhausted and dehydrated, he turned the wrong way. Officials set him off in the right direction but he fell several times more before being helped across the line. John Rodda surmised: "The fact that like many competitors he had taken some form of strychnine was a contributory factor."

(It's often said that Arthur Conan Doyle, writer of the *Sherlock Holmes* novels, was among those who helped him over the line. Doyle, in fact, was in the stands. His report in the *Daily Mail* confirmed that: "Then he collapsed... *within a few yards of my seat.*")

Next in was Johnny Hayes, an American who came second. This was the year the American team was led by the ever-protesting James E. Sullivan, the man behind the mud-throwing and tree-climbing in St.

Les Woodland

Louis. And Sullivan protested. His man had run all the way unaided and the Italian would still have been flat on the floor if supposedly neutral officials hadn't pulled him up, he said. Or shouted.

Well, he had a good point and the judges could see it, although only after a long time spent with conflicting arguments. In the end, Hayes was made the winner and the unfortunate Pietri was scrubbed from the results. The Italian was the race hero, though, and Queen Alexandra gave him an enormous gold cup for his bravery. Conan Doyle was among those who contributed.

Pietri took several days to recover and was said, perhaps fancifully, to have displaced his heart several centimeters. Not that that stopped his going off on an exhibition tour of America, sometimes running again against Hayes, and where he won so many hearts that Irving Berlin wrote a song about him, his first hit. It was called Dorando and, er, didn't exactly ignore the runner's accent. The verse starts:

> *Dorando! Dorando!*
> *He run-a, run-a, run-a, run like anything*
> *One-a, two-a hundred times around da ring*
> *I cry, "Please-a nunga stop!"*
> *Just then, Dorando he's a drop!*

Pietri may not have been a shining, pure amateur. He collected £300, a lot of money in 1908, from a public appeal in Britain and a great deal more in race contracts in the USA. The British fund had been to set him up as a baker in Italy. But he stayed on in England and ran a hotel in Birmingham. The business failed and he returned to Italy. He still had the Queen's cup but he kept it in a bank vault. He died when he was 56.

Five Things You Didn't Know You Didn't Know...About Track And Field

1. Jefferson Perez Quezada won Ecuador's first gold medal, in 1996. For winning the walk, he received free yogurt for life.

2. The first 13 ancient Olympics had only a sprint—the length of the stadium at Olympia, 192 meters. The first winner was a cook, Coroebus of Elis, in 776 BCE.

3. The idea of all the Olympic competitors mixing together at the closing ceremony came from an Australian teenager, Ian Wing, and happened for the first time at Melbourne.

4. Spiridon Louis, winner of the first modern marathon, presented Adolf Hitler with an olive branch from Olympia at the start of the 1936 Games in Berlin as a symbol of peace and friendship.

5. Prince George of Greece ran beside Louis as he won the marathon in 1896. When he asked him what he would like as a prize, the winner said he'd like a horse and cart for those in his village to take water to Athens, where the supply was poor.

Les Woodland

12

How Not To Fly The Flag

Those 1908 Games were in trouble from the start. The newspaper magnate, Lord Northcliffe, had to bail them out with £12,000. But it was the first to restrict entries, and the first at which the Americans refused to dip their flag as they passed the King's saluting base.

"This flag dips to no earthly king," said the flag's bearer.

But who was he, why did he do it, and did he actually say it? Bill Mallon and Ian Buchanan of the grandly named International Society of Olympic Historians say three flag-bearers have been suggested—Ralph Rose, Martin Sheridan and Johnny Garrells—but that "without doubt" it was Rose. They quote numerous reports from the era saying so. But none of them mentions the "no earthly king" comment.

The reports say Garrells explained that he hadn't known what to do. That's possible but improbable given that the team had agreed to abide by the rules, which were also printed in newspapers, and that there had been two rehearsals in which Garrells would have seen what other teams did. Several reports of the time say that all countries lowered the flag. And none of the British papers mentioned an American affront to the king.

The flags had to be lowered twice, once on a march-past and then again when teams lined up before the Royal Box. It's unlikely British papers would have missed the Stars and Stripes flying high while all the others were lowered, so perhaps it had happened during the march-past and been missed.

If the "no earthly king" was ever uttered then it's not true that it started a tradition. American newspaper reports of 1924 make no mention of the flag not being dipped with all the others. And in 1932 the flag was undeniably dipped to Franklin D. Roosevelt, who admittedly was never a king, because the New York Times reported the event next day. Not until 1924 did it become a legal offense to lower the flag "to any person or thing."

As for the protest that "this flag dips to no earthly king," the words saw the light only long afterwards. It has become a legend that has become fact.

It's true, however, that the American and Swedish flags had been accidentally omitted from those around the stadium before the opening ceremony. Both nations were cross but the legend that the Swedish team or just its wrestlers pulled out in protest is also untrue; Sweden competed throughout the Games. Curiously, though, the Chinese and Japanese flags were there even though neither was competing.

Flags were a repeated problem; Finland chose to carry none rather than the flag of the Soviet Union (of which it was unwillingly part), and some Irish competitors withdrew rather than march behind the Union Flag of Great Britain, a country they considered an occupying power.

London was the Games where the American manager, James Sullivan, made close on one official complaint a day. His most striking one came in the athletics and undermined the view of Olympic authorities generally and de Coubertin specifically that judges in all Games should be British. They believed in the natural fairness of Englishmen and they approved the ethics of the private school system which de Coubertin admired so much.

Sullivan didn't agree. The incident that made him most bitter concerned an aristocratic Englishman called Wyndham Halswelle, in the final of the 400-meter on July 23. Halswelle—born Mayfair, London, on May 30, 1882, educated Charterhouse and Sandhurst army college—was lined up against three Americans, John Carpenter of Cornell University, William Robbins of Harvard, and John Taylor of the University of Pennsylvania.

The four came into the final straight and Halswelle tried to take the lead. At that moment Carpenter moved out and blocked him. Carpenter was accused of obstructing Halswelle deliberately and the race was scheduled to be rerun two days later. Only Halswelle turned up. The Americans had refused to compete. They said no obstruction had taken place; the British said it had. Both countries had different rules and each was right under those it followed. The debate grew into a row and American officials were ordered off the track. It was after that that the IOC decided it wouldn't have just British judges after all and, from London onwards, it appointed judges from across the world. It was also then that sports began to adopt standardized rules.

Halswelle, incidentally, never recovered from the incident. He made a final appearance at the Glasgow Rangers Sports that same year—his family was Scottish—and never ran again. He was killed by a sniper at the Battle of Neuve Chappelle in France in March 1915.

• • •

Pierre de Coubertin first spoke the words "the most important thing in the Olympic Games is not to win but to take part... not to have conquered but to have fought well" at a service in St. Paul's cathedral, London, on July 19, 1908. He didn't invent them, however. In his speech he credited a sermon by the Bishop of Pennsylvania a few days earlier.

13

How To Lack The Olympic Spirit (1)

The Olympic Games are awarded not to a country but to a city. The idea was to avoid nationalism, although it was a vain hope that died when the Germans turned their Games into a showroom for the Nazi ideal.

Giving the Games to a city, however much the pitch may be made by a national Olympics committee, means that they are in the end subject to the city's mayor and its voters. Which is how it is that in 1971 Denver, Colorado, pulled out of running a Games which only the previous year it had agreed to hold. Environmental campaigners and conservationists were so angry about the damage they predicted would be done to the beauty and natural peace of the Rockies that they forced the city to change its mind.

The journalist John Rodda said the relationship from the start between the summer and winter Olympics "has at the best been uneasy, at the worst barely tolerable." Winter sports appeared for the first time when figure skating was included in the London Olympics of 1908. Scandinavia had dominated cross-country skiing. Norway, which held a Nordic Games on a four-year cycle like the Olympics, saw itself the spiritual home of faster, higher and further through the snow.

Then in 1911 an Englishman, Henry Lunn, invented downhill racing and the slalom. Lunn was a Methodist missionary in India until he fell too ill to continue. He had never been to Switzerland but, in retirement, he decided it was just the place to promote a conference to unite Christendom.

"At the end of the conference," he said in mock sadness, "I found myself £500 in pocket." It was a huge sum in 1892 and Lunn thought he could do better. But knowing a bit about the moneyed classes of

Les Woodland

Britain, he knew they would see it below themselves to sign up with a mere "travel agent." What he needed was a better name. So he opened the Public Schools Alpine Sports Club, a public school in Britain being not what it is elsewhere but one that charges fees for a private education.

His grandson, Peter Lunn, said he was then able to book whole hotels, "so that his clientele could practice winter sports abroad in the serene confidence that they would find among their fellow guests no foreigners and no Englishmen who were not of the right class." The appeal was immediate and Lunn booked so many hotels that the Swiss themselves were kept out. And to entertain his snooty guests one day in 1903, he organized a snow triathlon: skiing (walking round a field), skating and toboggan. By 1911 the other events were dropped and walking round a field turned into a downhill race. A sport had been born.

The first recognized winter Games were at Chamonix, France, in 1924. Trouble started almost immediately, not least professionalism. Rows went on and reached a deafening point when an American millionaire, Avery Brundage, became president of the International Olympic Committee. He flew into a rage when he thought he'd been promised that skiers would wear no advertising at Grenoble in 1968. Instead, they not only had the maker's name prominently written on their skis but they held up their skis to show it the moment a camera appeared.

In 1972 the Austrian skier, Karl Schranz, was already in the Olympic village when Brundage—who said he had a blacklist of 40 prime offenders—had him disqualified because he was making thousands of dollars a year from the sport. He was the "most blatant and the most verbose [offender] we could find."

Rodda said: "While skiing caused the IOC much concern, the Olympic skating rinks were used by some individuals to raise their contractual price for ice shows, once they had won their Olympic medal."

The German skater, Katarina Witt, turned up with a bare bottom to skate in 1968 and was sent away to cover it with feathers. The incident did no harm in securing a contract to pose in *Playboy*.

The Olympics' 50 Craziest Stories

Rodda continued: "The expensive installation of bob runs at winter Games sites, for what is a little-practiced sport, was criticized for being against the Olympic rule that a sport must be widely engaged in." It was a point that Squaw Valley, in the USA, could see when in 1960 it simply refused to build them, even though the entrepreneurs behind the Games had created an entire sports resort where previously there had been just a single hotel.

Denver's decision to drop the 1976 Games weakened the winter Olympics still further. Some forecast it would spell their end.

Denver had won the IOC's consent over Sion in Switzerland, Tampere in Finland and Whistler, in western Canada. It had barely happened when environmentalists and politicians, including the future governor, Dick Lamm, protested. Their cause was helped when the expected cost rose 300 per cent.

Denver planned to raise the money by issuing bonds worth $5 million. That added to worries that the beauty of the Rockies would be permanently scarred by installations and stadiums whose glory would die the day the Games ended. There was the further consideration that the best snow was on the west of the Rockies, whereas Denver was on the east. The grass was literally greener on Denver's side of the mountain because February, the planned date, was warm enough to walk and pick flowers. The IOC, its knowledge of American geology and meteorology slight, hadn't thought of that. Nor had the promoters made a lot of it.

The organizers were therefore faced with creating artificial snow for a whole mountainside, using 17 million gallons of water a night. They would also have to bulldoze much of it for ski runs and jumps. They had promised that the Games would be within 45 minutes' drive from the city. That meant slopes that ski specialists had rejected as inadequate. But still more concerned were the well-heeled people of Evergreen, a suburb surrounded by parkland. They spotted that the cross-country routes ran through their gardens and a school. The Games vice-president acknowledged that was just about right, although "the trails are only eight feet wide and don't go through any buildings—just backyards and the Wilmot school yard. Some people would have to let us put gaps in their fences."

Les Woodland

Things were turning absurd. Colorado, which had backed the Games, got cold feet. Its tourist industry depends on its beautiful skiing. It shrank at the thought of the world seeing snow machines working on bare hillsides.

In November 1972, voters rejected the idea with the argument that no public money could be spent. The Games were abandoned and given to Innsbruck, which had never asked for them. And to complete the embarrassment, Beaver Creek resort, where the alpine events were to have been, was built nevertheless. The roads around it, said *Sports Illustrated*, are choked beyond the worst predictions of 1972.

• • •

Anders Haugen of the USA came fourth in the ski jumping in 1924. It took 50 years to realize he should have been third. The judges had miscounted. Haugen, then 83, flew to Oslo and collected his bronze medal.

14

How To Lack The Olympic Spirit (2)

Jamie Salé and David Pelletier were so flawless in the free skating at Salt Lake City—this is another winter Olympics story—that the crowd went wild. The two Canadians finished their routine and loosened up by skating round the track as their fans demanded the maximum score by chanting: "Six! Six!"

And then the judges gave the gold to the Russian team of Elena Berezhnaya and Anton Sikharulidze.

This would have been surprising anyway but it was stunning after Sikharulidze had flopped a double-Axel. But it wasn't the way the judges saw it and four of them put the Russians ahead of the Canadians.

American and Canadian commentators on television had picked Salé and Pelletier as winners even before their routine had ended. They were outraged and they referred to one woman in particular: Marie-Reine Le Gougne of France.

Sally-Anne Stapleford, the British former international who was head of the technical committee, was waiting when Le Gougne got to the lobby of her hotel. Would she, Stapleford asked, say if there was more to the voting than there should have been?

Le Gougne burst into tears. A story emerged that the French skating administration had done a deal with Russia. If Russia won the free skating, France would win the dance. It was the story she repeated to fellow judges next day, but then she contradicted some parts and retracted others. Eventually she said things had happened the other way round: that the Russians were better but that she'd been urged to vote for the Canadians.

Le Gougne and the head of the French federation were both suspended for three years. The International Skating Union said it would investigate but little came of it. There was too little evidence

Les Woodland

of a deal with the Russians. Jacques Rogge, the head of the IOC, intervened and Salé and Pelletier's silver medal was exchanged for gold. The Russians kept their gold medal and so two pairs won.

Nobody but the Canadians came out of it well. Stapleford lost her seat on the technical committee of the international skating federation in the row that followed. She and others founded a rival, the World Skating Federation. It was to overthrow the ISU but it couldn't. Stapleford and her colleagues were thrown out of the sport by the ISU or their national federations.

The FBI suspected a Russian gangster, Alimzhan Tokhtakhounov, who was also close to tennis players. Italian police arrested him but let him go when extradition failed. By then phone taps suggested that the French dancer, Marina Anissina, knew a fix was taking place. She denied it, although she said she knew Tokhtakhounov and spoke to him by phone "from time to time."

Anissina was Russian by birth. Her mother also knew Tokhtakhounov.

This, you'd think, was as much of a scandal as the winter Olympics needed. But things were still worse in 1994.

Two American women were rivals for the gold medal at Lillehammer, in Norway. In some ways they were similar, in other ways a contrast. Tonya Harding's father was often out of work; her mother made her skating costumes but, Harding said, often physically abused her—a claim the mother denies. Nancy Kerrigan's father worked as a welder and supported his daughter's skating by working three jobs and dressing the ice at the local ice rink in exchange for her lessons. Kerrigan had class and Harding was the rough kid from the other end of town.

Harding's supporters doubted her talent. If they couldn't be sure she'd win the national championship, some decided they'd bludgeon Kerrigan to lessen the opposition. A thug, Shane Stant, therefore attacked Kerrigan as she was practicing. He didn't succeed in breaking her leg but he did bruise her enough above the knee to force her out of the championship. Harding took the title instead and she had her ticket for Lillehammer.

Kerrigan, though, recovered and she too was selected.

꿔

Stant, it emerged, had been employed by Harding's former husband, Jeff Gillooly, and her bodyguard, Shawn Eckardt. It's not clear how much Harding knew and, without evidence, selectors backed down from deselecting her when she threatened to sue. Kerrigan came second in Lillehammer and Harding finished eighth.

Gillooly, Stant, Eckardt and a getaway driver all went to jail. Harding admitted hampering their prosecution and was given three years' probation, fined $160,000 and told to do 500 hours of community service. The American skiing association banned her from competing as an amateur and professionals on the ice-show circuit refused to work with her.

Her troubles didn't end there. A video of her and Gillooly having sex appeared on the internet and stills from it were published in *Penthouse*. Her attempts to become a musician ended when her band was booed off stage in its only performance. Money became tight and she took up boxing. She stopped after six fights.

Kerrigan, on the other hand, turned professional and danced in ice shows. She graduated from a business college and works now for her own charity for the blind. She was inducted into American skating's Hall of Fame in 2004.

Harding wasn't.

• • •

Russia's Evgeni Plushenko, a figure skater not known for humility, climbed on the top rung of the podium in Vancouver even though he'd come second. "I felt that I'd stepped on to my position. It wasn't planned, of course. It's just that in my brain, I'd won," he said. Vladimir Putin, supported him: "Your silver is as good as gold," he said. Not for Plushenko it wasn't; his website says he won *platinum*.

Les Woodland

Five Things You Didn't Know You Didn't Know... About The Winter Olympics

1. Antoine Millordos of Greece fell 18 times during the slalom in the 1952 Games.

2. The South Korean, Kyung Soon-Yil, said he had never skied in his life before the Games at Squaw Valley in 1960.

3. Resat Erces set a record difficult to beat by averaging just 9 kilometers per hour in the downhill in 1936.

4. Diana Gordon-Lennox skied in a monocle and with one leg in plaster in 1936.

5. Marja Liisa Hämäläinen of Finland won three cross-country skiing medals in 1984 but was so shy that she hid after each victory rather than meet journalists.

15

How To Go On And On And On

There is, shall we say, a certain intimacy in wrestling. It is one of the world's few permissible ways of getting into instant skin-touching contact with a sweaty stranger and stay locked together for ages. But some people have taken this closeness too far.

Wrestling may attract only other wrestlers as spectators but it's one of the Games' classic sports, there right back in the original days and therefore featured again when de Coubertin revived the Games in Athens in 1896. All sports learn as they go along, of course, and what wrestling learned was that it needed a way to stop bouts going on for ever if neither wrestler could be pinned to the ground.

This came especially obvious when Max Klein and Alpo Asikainen wrestled for a numbing 11 hours and 40 minutes at Stockholm in 1912. The need for each to win had a political aspect. Klein was Estonian and Asikainen Finnish. Finland and Estonia were occupied by the USSR. But while Finns has been allowed to compete under their own flag, Klein had been obliged to compete for the Russian Empire. The bout was therefore described as "hostile."

The two fought on, ever more weary, for half a day. The sun shone on them from an uninterrupted sky. They stopped not every few minutes, like boxers, but every half an hour. After a drink, they went back into combat. Klein finally pinned Asikainen to the canvas but both men were so exhausted that losing was as much a relief as winning.

Klein was so shattered that he had no strength left for the final the following day. He gave up there and then and the gold medal went without a fight to Claes Johansson of Sweden. Only in 1918, with the birth of the Estonian Republic, was Klein acknowledged to have been not Russian but Estonian. He was therefore the little Baltic nation's first Olympic medalist.

"It was an important factor in our national awakening," says the Estonian Institute. He also became the first Estonian sportsman mentioned in the *Guinness Book of Records*. His exhausting 12 hours of wrestling may now be forgotten elsewhere but it remains a world record. And always will because the wrestling world couldn't face its happening again and brought in points scoring.

(Wrestling wasn't the only sport where conflict between the USSR and its satellites came to the fore. The water-polo semifinal between Hungary and the Russians in 1956 ended prematurely after a battle of kicks and punches. Hungary was leading and was given the victory.)

Things went on for almost as long in the heavyweight wrestling— and just as oddly. The final was between Anders Ahlgren of Sweden and Ivar Bohling of Finland. This time the two fought for nine hours. They'd have gone on longer had the judges not ruled that neither looked like beating the other and gave not a gold but a silver medal to both of them.

The wrestlers had the advantage of being on two legs. Cyclists have to compete on two wheels.

Now, bicycle sprinting isn't just blasting for the line. The sprint is only 200 meters long, but it's so important to be in the right position that the riders have four times as far to play cat and mouse. The rider in front has an advantage—because he's in front—but he can't see his rival. The rival is behind but he has the benefit of surprise. And whoever rides behind the other in the final dash has the benefit of his rival's slipstream. But he has, of course, to get past the leader. Not every rider has the same preference, hence the cat-and-mouse.

A rider with good balance can alternate the pressure on his pedals and stand still. Pierre Trentin and Giovanni Pettenella were so anxious to bluff each other into a disadvantageous position that in 1964 they balanced for 22 minutes. And then the Italian beat the Frenchman.

Pettenella later did better and stood still for an hour and five minutes in the Italian championship. It's a record not likely to be beaten. A history says: "In Varese on that hot August day in 1968 the commentator covering the event for Italian national television ran out of people to interview, and a crowd of curious spectators slowly

ɚ

started flocking to the velodrome to witness the event." His rival, Sergio Bianchetto, collapsed unconscious.

• • •

Christa Luding-Rothenburger of East Germany won silver in the cycling sprint in Seoul. She'd won gold and silver in speed skating that February. She will always be the only athlete to win medals at the summer and winter Games in the same year, because the Games are now in different years.

Les Woodland

16

How To Give Sex A Bad Name

Dora Ratjen wasn't the best high-jumper Germany could pick for the Berlin Olympics but she did come fourth. And two years later she set a world record. The only problem was that Dora was a man.

This bizarre story starts in the political atmosphere of the Berlin Games of 1936. The first choice to win the high-jump for Hitler's Germany was a 20-year-old called Gretel Bergmann. The letter that arrived at her home in Laupheim, in the southwest, began, like all official letters, with "Heil Hitler!" It told her she would compete in the Olympics, which didn't surprise her because she was the best in Germany. She had won the Olympic trials, after all.

Then, two weeks before the Games, Germany dropped her because of "mediocre performance." She was Jewish but that wasn't mentioned. She was to be replaced by a member of the Hitler Youth, a girl called Dora Ratjen who had a deep voice, stubble and was said never to take communal showers. She went to the Games and came fourth.

Ratjen's family near Bremen were described as "simple folk." The midwife who attended the birth called out "It's a boy!" Then she changed her mind and called the child a girl. The family named her Dora and brought her up as a girl. Then puberty came and Dora realized she could be a boy. She was too embarrassed to talk about it.

Dora and Bergmann met when they became talented jumpers. They even shared a room. Bergmann said: "I never had any suspicions, not even once... In the communal shower we wondered why she never showed herself naked. It was grotesque that someone could still be that shy at the age of 17. We just thought, 'She's strange. She's odd'... But no-one knew or noticed anything about her different sexuality."

Dora strapped up her genitals for Berlin but just missed a medal. She won the European championship in Vienna. Then something just as odd happened. She was taking a train from Vienna to Cologne when the conductor told police he had seen a man dressed as a woman. She had five o'clock shadow. Dora showed her papers identifying her as a woman but the police remained suspicious. They took her to Hohenlychen hospital, where doctors were as uncertain as the midwife.

Fraud proceedings began but were dropped "because there was no intention to reap financial reward." Dora promised not to take part in sport again. Her father still thought of her as a girl but in March 1939 he told police in Bremen: "Following the change of the register office entry regarding the child's sex, I would request you change the child's first name to Heinrich."

Athletics scrubbed her from the records. Nothing more was heard of her. Then in 1957 a barman in Hamburg said he was Dora Ratjen. He called himself Hermann now. He had been Dora for only three years—until the fuss about the Games was over, presumably, although it's not clear—a period he described, according to Time, as "most dull." It was the Nazis who spotted the potential of a man who might pass as a woman, he said, and he was told to take part "or else."

Less colorful but more probable is that Dora was the victim of an unworldly family, an embarrassed era, a difficult situation, and a sequence of events that got out of control.

He—or she—died aged 90 without giving another interview.

And then there was Stella the Fella.

Stella Walsh was born Stanislawa Walasiewiczowna in Poland in 1911. Her family, which called her Stasia, emigrated to Cleveland in the USA when she was three months old. There her parents simplified her name. She became Stella Walsh.

She showed early talent—she beat 20 records and won 41 national championships—but she couldn't compete for the USA without becoming American. And she couldn't do that until she was 21. She never forgot that America, the only country she'd known, had made her wait. She was on the verge of taking citizenship so she could be in the US team in Los Angeles in 1932, then pulled out and confirmed her Polish nationality instead.

In Los Angeles she equaled the world record for 100 meters in the heats, the semifinal and the final, which she won. She then won nine

Les Woodland

gold medals at the Championships of Warsaw and in Poznan she broke two world records in the same day. She was voted Poland's most popular athlete in three successive years.

Her dreams of settling in Poland ended with German and then Russian invasion in the war. She retired from international athletics after the Berlin Olympics in 1936 and became American in 1947. She married a boxer, Neil Olson—although they separated after eight weeks—and won her last American title when she was 40, in 1951.

In December, 1980, she was outside a shopping mall in Cleveland, a bystander at a holdup. She was shot dead. Her body was taken for an autopsy and there surgeons found she had male and female chromosomes and male genitalia. She was Stella the Fella.

A recreation center in Cleveland is named after her and she is buried in the city's Calvary cemetery.

• • •

Mary Louise Edith Weston—"the Devonshire Wonder"—won the British shot, javelin and discus championships in 1929. A little later she had "a series of operations in Charing Cross hospital" as the papers of the era put it delicately and reemerged as Mark and worked as a masseur. His sister, Hilda, had a similar operation and became Harry, although he killed himself in 1942 "depressed following [his] operations for change of sex."

In 1938 Mark married a longtime friend, Alberta Bray, a "shy blonde in her early twenties."

• • •

The Dutch runner Amelia Louer-Hinton went to the sex test at Mexico and heard the shocking words: "We have something serious to tell you." Her face whitened. Then the medical crew told her: "Congratulations! You're going to have a baby." Louer-Hinton, who withdrew from the 400 meters, said: "I was amazed. I had no idea I was going to be a mother."

17

How To Make A Runner Run

Haiti is a poor country with an unhappy history. Its people have enough to do without worrying about sport and anyway there's little money to send teams abroad. Haiti took part in the Olympics twice in the 1920s—its rifle-shooting team won in 1924 and Silvio Cater came second in the high jump in 1928—and once in the 1930s. Nothing then until 1960 and nothing after that before 1972.

From 1972 Haiti competed more frequently and in 1976 it sent Dieudonné Lamothe to Montreal. There he ran the 5,000-meter. The gold medal went, as predicted to Lasse Viren, the "flying Finn" as reporters called him. But the darling of the crowd was Lamothe, who led the first lap of his heat and then grew so tired that he finished five minutes after the rest.

"For Haiti, I have given it my all like my life depended on it," he said. It was hard not to like him. But nobody then realized that he may have been talking literally...

Haiti sent him to run the marathon in Los Angeles in 1984. He once more finished last, now happier than ever. Not because his time had changed the world, because 2 hours 52 minutes 18 seconds was half an hour outside the record. The gold medalist would have had time to shower and eat a meal before Lamothe came in. No, Lamothe was happy because Haiti's murderous dictator, Bébé Doc Duvalier, had promised to kill him if he didn't finish.

With Jean-Claude Duvalier, nobody knew. His eccentricity and bloodlust knew no limit. Word had it that he once gave Olympic selections to two airport workers simply because they had pleased him. What difference the threat made, only Lamothe knew. But he ran and he ran the best he could.

Les Woodland

Haiti overthrew Duvalier in 1986 and Lamothe went to Seoul in 1988 in far better mood. There he ran 2 hours 16 minutes 15 seconds, two minutes outside his best, and came 20th. His last Olympics was Barcelona, in 1992, where he finished the marathon in 2 hours 36 minutes 11 seconds at the age of 37. He won the Francophone Games and in 1996 he won the Long Island marathon in the USA. He still holds Haitian records for the marathon—2 hours 14 minutes 22 seconds in 1988—and for 5,000-meter: 15 minutes 33.26 seconds, set the following year.

Anecdote: a young Haitian cyclist, Philippe Dumoulin, was having a hard time while training in a group riding at 40 kilometers per hour. The cycling team often passed Lamothe, running alone, during their sessions. Dumoulin was suffering and dropped off the group. Lamothe ran up behind him, continued a little further, then ran back.

"Are you unwell?" he asked.

"No," Dumoulin answered, "just shattered."

"You've got all evening to feel like that," came the sharp response, "but you've only got two hours for training. Don't confuse the two. Just because you're tired, you're wasting your time and you're wasting mine."

Dumoulin took in the words but still felt bad.

"It's hard to be the first to be dropped from the group."

Lamothe laughed.

"I have to train alone and nobody's there to encourage me. There's not even an athletics federation to support me. You, you can carry a bottle of water on your bike and I can't do even that. You have a car and a coach to follow you on the road, but I don't. The essential rule you've got to remember, in running like in cycling, is that what's important is not to win but to be able to cover the distance and cross the finish line. Even if you don't win in front of everybody, you have that unbeatable sensation inside you that you've won because you finished the course."

Dumoulin was inspired and won the national championship for his age group.

18

How Not To Use Your Brain

It seemed such a good wheeze. The Paralympics, the Games for the disabled, are coming up. You decide to enter a team that will win a gold medal. And you use the success to wring more money from the government and anyone else.

There's just one problem. You have to be sure of a winning team. If you don't have that guarantee, you're just one more country among many.

Well, the Spanish hit on the answer. They'd enter a team for Sydney that could act disabled even if they weren't. They couldn't hide having the right number of arms or legs or that they weren't in wheelchairs. But they could pose as mentally handicapped. There was a category for that.

And so in October 2000, Spain beat Russia 87-63 in the final of the basketball. It was just one more victory in Spain's progress to third most successful nation. And nobody need ever know.

Except that someone did know. Carlos Ribagorda had been in the team for two years, and Ribagorda was a journalist with a business magazine, *Capital*. The name is a play on words, referring both to money and to Madrid, where it was published. Ribagorda collected his gold medal along with the others, then blew the gaff in his magazine.

There had, he said, been two handicapped players in the team. But the rest were quite normal and had been taken on just to be sure of a medal. More exciting still, it hadn't been the first time. Spain won the basketball world championship in Brazil with four players with no disability. And there were suspicions about Spain's athletics team, two swimmers and a table-tennis player.

Attention turned on Fernando Vicente Martin, a bigwig in the world of disabled sport, the father of a disabled daughter and vice-president of the Spanish Paralympic Committee. He insisted the team had been genuine, that every player was below the IQ limit of 75. Ribagorda, he was quoted as saying, was "a handicapped person who has gone mad."

But they were the protests of a condemned man. The paralympic committee investigated and Martin was expelled. The international organization took a closer look at the registration forms from around the world and found 14 missing. Of the remaining 219, no fewer than 157—almost three in four—were found to be unsatisfactory, information not given or not given completely. The 157 invalid entries accounted for 94 of the 132 medals won. An invalid entry didn't mean the athlete was a cheat but each one spoke of how poor were the checks on who was entering and what had been claimed.

The result was embarrassing. The Spanish gave back their gold medals and sports for the mentally disabled—the "intellectually disabled", as they were officially called—were suspended while one attempt after another at writing a definition and finding a test failed.

• • •

The Paralympic Games have their root in rehabilitation of British soldiers after the second world war. Sir Ludwig Guttman organized a competition between hospitals to coincide with the 1948 Olympics in London. The challenge ran annually and became the Stoke Mandeville Games after the treatment center at the national spinal injuries center near Aylesbury which he ran north of the capital.

Guttman took the Stoke Mandeville Games to the 1960 Olympics in Rome and promoted events for 400 disabled athletes. They became the Paralympic Games. Guttman, a German neurologist who'd fled the Nazis in 1939, died in 1980.

19

How To Give The Olympics A Bad Name

It's not easy to find what people thought of the Berlin Olympics at the time. Most of the disapproving accounts are written afterwards, with hindsight not only of the Games but of the history that followed.

There had, said the veteran newspaper reporter Peter Wilson, been calls from Jewish and American organizations to have the Games moved elsewhere, but that is hardly unusual. Someone *always* objects, right up to modern times. Ask the Chinese. When it's not about politics or civil rights, it follows stories that a Games will be chaotically organized or, thanks to grave financial problems, not take place at all.

Hitler in 1936 was new on the scene. The Games had been awarded to Germany before his rise to the top and his establishment of a Nazi state. But he made the most of it. Wilson, who remembered that from his hotel room he could see photos of Hitler, Goering and Goebbels, explained how different the world was then.

"In 1936 there were few dictatorships. The Spanish Civil War had been in progress only two weeks by the time the Games started in Berlin on August 1. Italy had long been under the domination of Benito Mussolini, destined to turn out a sawdust Caesar. But you needed visas, as far as I know, for no European countries apart from Russia—and you never met anyone who had been to the USSR. But we had read accounts of German anti-Semitism and of its corollary, a color bar which was second only in viciousness to that in force, at the time, in the Deep South of the United States."

In other words, not only were many praising Hitler for bringing order to Germany, for showing a new way and for holding back communism, but there was worse in Arkansas. That's why you have to be careful of reports written afterwards. They have the benefit of knowing how history turned out. Those who praised Hitler and those who prolonged suppression of blacks in the US long after the war ended were horribly, horribly wrong. But that doesn't make all the reports of the Berlin Olympics true.

It's true that Goebbels wrote in *Der Angriff* that American black athletes were merely the team's "black auxiliaries" and it's true that he didn't include their medals in the paper's score chart. But it's not true that Hitler walked out of the stadium when Jesse Owens won yet again. And it's not true that he refused specifically to congratulate him.

On the first day Hitler invited three medal winners to his box for public congratulation: a Finn and two Germans—the javelin-thrower Tilly Fleischer and the shot-putter Hans Woellke.

Richard D. Mandell, in *The Nazi Olympics*, said the IOC president, Henri de Baillet-Latour, then "sent word to Hitler that he was merely a guest of honor at the Games. He should congratulate all or none. He chose to congratulate none—in public at least. Thereafter, he did warmly felicitate German victors, in private however."

It was from there that grew the myth of Jesse Owens. It says that Hitler refused to congratulate him because he was black. At first Owens tried to keep the record straight—in fact, he said, Hitler had waved to him and smiled—but eventually he went along with the myth and profited from it.

He needed the money, any money, because there were none of the advertising contracts and generous endorsement deals accorded to modern winners. Owens was black and he wasn't invited to the White House, where an election was being planned: seeing the president congratulating a black man could wreck the vote in the South. Owens became a bankrupt within three years.

Owens didn't win his first medal until the second day, by which time Hitler had had his warning. Owens wasn't congratulated because Hitler was no longer congratulating anybody. The belief that Hitler was so displeased to see Owens win that he marched out of the stadium in a temper has its origin in unscrupulous editing of newsreel film. The unedited version shows Hitler as excited about black athletes as white ones. As was the crowd, which shouted Owens' name and stopped

ॐ

him so often in the street for autographs that he complained. Owens'
biographer, William J. Baker, said American newspapers—in those
years in a ruthless circulation war—made up the story of Hitler's snub.

The incident in which Hitler walked out of the stadium concerned
another black American. Cornelius Johnson won the first gold medal
for America that first day and could have received his medal from
Hitler. But Hitler left the stadium as the medal presentation began, a
government spokesman saying he had long been scheduled to leave
at that time to go to another appointment. Whether that was true or
not, the fact is that the medalist was Johnson and not Owens. When
Owens became the American hero of the Games, the incident got
transferred to him.

Goebbels and the Nazis didn't see black success as embarrassing
to their theories, because they simply ignored it. That was why black
athletes weren't included in the medal tables. But there had been
many more white winners than black and that, for the Nazis, proved
the superiority of the white race.

Wilson praises the colossal scale of Berlin, the first to be televised,
where bulletins were distributed in 14 languages and where no fewer
than 10,000 people were involved in a single festival play on the Games'
periphery.

But, he said: "Sadly, though, the overall memory of the 1936 Games
was the *Deutschland über alles* atmosphere engendered by Hitler and
the Nazis. Everywhere the eye was affronted by flags upon flags, bearing
the crooked cross; everywhere the ear was assailed by loudspeakers
playing martial music or relaying the hysterical *Sieg heil* responses
of the thoughtless multitudes to the appearance of the Führer. There
have been other Games where tragedy has intruded—but never again,
I hope, will there be a world festival of sport where the prevailing air
was so odiously chauvinistic and military."

When the Third Reich ended, the Russians sent the entire executive
of the Games to a prison camp.

• • •

The world knows what happened to Hitler. But what happened to
Owens? He had ticker-tape parades but never a letter of congratulations

Les Woodland

from the president, Franklin D. Roosevelt. There was little he could live on. He became bankrupt after three years and picked up money where he could, including racing against a horse. He moved to Chicago in 1949, started a public relations firm and presented a radio jazz show. He died, a heavy smoker, of lung cancer in 1980. He was 66.

And the man he beat? Germany's hope had been a giant Aryan, 19-year-old Luz Long. Owens jumped 8.06 meters and Long 7.87. Recognizing he had been outclassed, Long walked to Owens and hugged him in congratulation. It was affection for a rival to whom he had also offered advice, but not a gesture appreciated in Nazi Germany.

Owens said: "It took a lot of courage for him to befriend me in front of Hitler... You can melt down all the medals and cups I have and they wouldn't be a plating on the 24-karat friendship that I felt for Luz Long at that moment."

Long died in a military hospital after defending Sicily against the British in 1943. Days earlier, he wrote to his old rival. He urged: "After the war, go to Germany. Find my son and talk to him of his father. Talk to him of a time when war didn't separate us, and tell him that things can be different between men on this Earth. Your brother, Luz."

Owens did meet Luz's son. They stood together in the Berlin stadium in 1962, Owens' arm around Kai's shoulder and Kai's around Owens'.

20

How To Do It On A Shoestring

The Games in 1947 were awarded to a bankrupt and bomb-wrecked Britain. The country was surviving on American aid negotiated by the economist, John Maynard Keynes. This was to be an austerity Games.

London was the first Games since the Hitler Olympics in Berlin. Now nobody knew where the ceremonial flag was. Nobody had thought to look. Belgium had handed it to Germany at the end of the 1932 Games in Antwerp and Berlin used it in 1936. But then it vanished in the confusion of the Red Army's advance. It would have been forgivable to have made another one but as it happened the British Army found not only the flag amid the rubble but also Berlin's guest book, which was displayed at the Victoria and Albert museum before being sent to the IOC in Lausanne.

Countries were warned there wasn't much food. Britain had more severe rationing in 1947 than during the war and athletes would get no more to eat than was allowed to a worker in heavy industry. Teams brought their own food and many countries made donations.

Organizing things on a shoestring brought other problems. Teams arriving by air were logged in by a schoolteacher and a handful of volunteers relying on a few telephones with no dialed connections outside London. Stewards were sent to airports, especially Heathrow (formally opened only in May that year) and to neighboring Northolt. But aircraft held more than a few dozen passengers in those days and competitors began turning up not in small groups or individually.

There were 81 groups at Heathrow alone, containing 1,913 people. Many came without anyone in London knowing they were due. Even when groups said which aircraft they would be on, it wasn't unusual to be substantially delayed, so that the organizers' buses were tied up for hours as they waited for them.

Les Woodland

The organizers persuaded the biggest airlines—BOAC, BEA, KLM and Sabena among them—to divert their coach services to central London to the hosting centers set up in the suburbs. Other airlines had to be met separately, though, and before long the Games refused to wait for any aircraft not operated by BOAC, the British Airways of its day. The British could be depended on to know who was on board and when they would arrive, but foreigners were less organized, the organizers claimed, and so anyone turning up on a foreign plane was to phone from the airport to say he was there. He could then wait while a bus made its way from the suburbs of West Drayton or Uxbridge to collect him.

Sometimes athletes turned up at airports nobody had imagined. One afternoon a group of Hungarians were approaching Northolt, where arrangements were being made for them to land. A bus was sent to meet them. It waited two hours. Then at 7 PM Northolt said the plane had been sent to Blackbushe, an old Spitfire airport on the other side of London and five times as far away. The bus was called back to the depot, officials searched their maps and the magnificently named Aldershot and District Traction Company was asked to send a bus. Another three hours passed.

Finally, at 10 PM—five hours after the original expected landing at Northolt—an official at Manston, 80 miles from Blackbushe, put through a long-distance call (about 50 miles) to say he had a load of Hungarians in his office and what was he supposed do with them? (Answer: "Transport Department at once telephoned the East Kent Road Car Company's garage at Herne Bay, and by 12:30 AM in the morning the coach and company were at their housing center at Hendon School.")

The mystery is not so much that the problem was solved with goodwill and telephoning but that the flight from Hungary could have taken so long. Assuming the Hungarians landed at Manston half an hour before the airport official phoned, the Hungarians had spent four and a half hours flying over and around London—half as long again as their original flight and longer than you'd expect an everyday small aircraft to have fuel.

Transporting world's athletes had taken a long time to arrange. Petrol had been rationed in September 1939 and would stay rationed until June 1950. It could take months to get a new car and so few people were expected to drive to Wembley that parking was left to the company that owned the car park there. Not much more room was needed. Officials of both the Games and individual sports had to use their own car, if they owned one, and that meant permission, from the Ministry of Fuel and Power, to use petrol.

As for spectators, the organizers arranged half-price fares on trains. They couldn't be so flippant with competitors and officials, though. The problem was that 6,000 was a large number to carry in a capital only just able to transport its own residents.

London Transport offered some double-decker buses provided they weren't driven outside the London region. That ruled out Bisley (shooting), Henley (rowing) and Torquay (yachting). The final deal was for 20 double-decker buses holding 56 passengers each, a dozen single-decker coaches for 30 passengers, and "reluctantly" 20 obsolete 20-seaters which London Transport considered in too poor shape for general service. There was never a seat for everyone who needed to travel.

Bob Maitland, a competitor in the cycling road race at Windsor, remembered: "Our manager was a guy called Frank Slemen, who was a Liverpool butcher. He knew nothing about road racing and he admitted it. We had to sign on a day before the race and any other manager would have insisted the other teams go to the British camp, not the other way round.

"So we went to the signing-on by bus and we all got seats except for one of our riders, who had to stand. Frank could see the officials on the bus all had seats. So he went to a Dutch official and said his rider was having to stand and asked this guy to give up his seat. Now, Frank was the strongest guy I've known and when the Dutchman hesitated, he grabbed him by the lapels, lifted him two feet in the air and dropped him on the floor."

The Metropolitan police made bus drivers follow set routes, as though they were in normal service. That concentrated traffic into corridors, making jams more likely. London Transport drivers hastily recruited to the Olympic team often didn't know where they were going. It took many hundreds of arrows fastened to lampposts to solve the problem.

Les Woodland

Not everyone was appreciative of this effort. A cycling official became overexcited in Windsor Park during the road race and pirated an eight-seat bus and tried to drive off in it. Competitors themselves drove off in two other buses, one in London and another at Henley. The London couple found themselves in somewhat lower spirits at Wembley police station a few hours later but there were no charges. The Henley joy-riders were never caught.

A bit of larking about was predictable. The consequences weren't as great, though, as a change of plan on Friday, July 30. The opening ceremony had been the previous day. That night the bus drivers had gone home with instructions to report to their accommodation centers in time to drive the wrestlers to the first event of the Games, their weigh-in at Earls Court in west London. It was after they clocked off that the organizers brought the weigh-in forward an hour.

It was rare to have a private telephone in 1948. The few who wanted one had to wait for months. The result was that the drivers couldn't be warned. Search parties had to be sent to their homes. Drivers who couldn't be found had to be replaced by others in hired cars and the bus drivers turned up at their depot to find their wrestlers gone.

21

How To Win The Hearts Of The World

Few swimming crowds have been more startled and then more enchanted than the day Eric the Eel struggled to stay above water. Because Eric had never raced more than 50 meters before his day of glory in Sydney in 2002.

Éric Moussambani, a 22-year-old from Equatorial Guinea, one of Africa's poorest and least developed countries, began swimming only the previous January. He found his place in the Olympics thanks to a lottery to allow places for athletes from undeveloped nations. The idea was to spread sport around the world. So Moussambani, who at home trained in a 20-meter hotel pool with no lane markers, carried the national flag in the opening ceremony and then went to the biggest pool he had ever seen. It must have looked terrifyingly long.

There, normally, he would have come last in his heat and been forgotten. But the two due to swim with him were disqualified for false starts and Moussambani swam alone.

"At first," said the man from the BBC, "those watching on thought nothing of the lazy-looking strokes, but after his 'interesting' flip turn at the halfway point, it suddenly became apparent this was no ordinary swim. Endeavoring to keep his head above water at all times and flailing his arms wildly, he somehow managed to stay afloat as he inched his way to the wall, and salvation. Once there, he held on for dear life, before emerging from the water to rapturous applause."

His time for 100 meters was 1 minute 52.72 seconds. It was not only more than a minute longer than the best—the winning time was 48.30—and 7 seconds longer than the world's best for twice as far. It was, though, a personal best—he had, after all, never swum so far before—and a national record for Equatorial Guinea.

"The last 15 meters were very difficult," he said.

Les Woodland

British newspapers revel in leg-pulling nicknames. The British ski-jumper Eddie Edwards, whose thick-lens glasses suggested he couldn't see even as far as the unimpressive leaps he made in 1988, became Eddie-the-Eagle. Moussambani became Eric-the-Eel thanks to an article by Craig Lord in the *London Times.*

"I want to send hugs and kisses to the crowd," Moussambani said after his trial of strength. "It was their cheering that kept me going."

He planned to swim again in 2004—he could by then swim twice as fast—but a visa mix-up kept him at home. He didn't swim in 2008, either, although a campaign started before the 2012 Games to see him swimming in London.

The attention and sympathy Moussambani attracted brought crowds of reporters to see Equatorial Guinea's only other swimmer, Paula Barila Bolopa. The London *Daily Telegraph* said: "The spectator gallery was almost full as the news spread that a female Eric was making an appearance."

The Times said: "Paula Barila Bolopa, still dripping wet from her swim, was under siege. Tape recorders were being thrust in her face and an interpreter was translating her comments from Spanish for American television stations. Somebody passed her a mobile phone so she could talk live to a radio presenter in Madrid and when she was asked whether she had signed any autographs since fame embraced her, she furrowed her brow in indignation. '*Muchos*,' she said. She and Celebrity had quickly become fast friends."

Barila Bolopa, a supermarket cashier when she wasn't swimming, showed the same courage and lack of talent as her teammate. She came last in her heat with 1 minute 3.97 seconds for 50 meters, twice as long as the next slowest. But like Eric the Eel, she had the hearts of the pool.

She said: "It's the first time I've swum 50 meters. It was further than I thought. I was very tired."

22

How To Be Disonischenko

Before we get to this story, consider the case of the Italian fencing team in Paris in 1924. They were so vexed by the Hungarian judges, and the judges by the Italians, that their row ended with a Hungarian coach challenging the Italian captain to a duel. Sword-fighters are well equipped to do this. And Paris between the wars was the sort of place where dueling was all but encouraged.

The challenge went ahead but spirits calmed when the Hungarian lunged and the Italian began bleeding. Enough was enough and honor had been settled.

Getting cross, though, can have other unusual consequences. The Soviet Union's volleyball team threatened to throw one of their country's pentathletes out of the window in 1976, for instance. It was as well they never met.

The man they wanted to defenestrate was an army officer called Boris Onishchenko—or Disonischenko as newspapers began to call him. He was one of the best in the world but a silver medal at Munich wasn't good enough. He wanted the gold medal four years later. To do that he had to be best overall in pistol shooting, swimming, show jumping, running and, significantly, with an epée.

Of all these, the sword fighting was the easiest to fix. In the old days, competitors shouted "Touché!" when they made or felt contact. By Montreal things were more sophisticated and a button in the tip of the epée clicked up the scoreboard with each touch instead.

Things came unraveled when Boris met Jim—his big rival from Britain, Jim Fox.

"What you have to remember is that I was very publicly a member of the British Army and Boris was a half-colonel in the KGB," Fox said. "It became a huge international incident. At one stage, I was told the

Les Woodland

whole Eastern bloc was going to pull out, and it was down to me. It's not ideal material for a competitor to be thinking about, is it?"

Fox was puzzled that Boris's sword had done no better than just swish through the air and yet his score had mounted. He'd seen the same when Boris had fenced against another Briton, Adrian Parker. Parker was a swimmer rather than a fencer and nobody had expected him to be anything but beaten. But the ease of the beating raised eyebrows.

When his own time came, Fox jumped so far backwards at Boris's first jab that the sword missed by a hand's length. It couldn't be mistaken, and yet still Boris scored a point. That was enough. British officials demanded to look at Onischenko's sword. And that was when Boris came closest to the salt mines. Because hidden inside the handle was a switch he could squeeze, a switch which would send a pulse down the cable that trailed behind him and bump up his score.

Neither the pentathlon in general or fencing in particular is a sport which attracts much attention when more popular events are going on elsewhere. But news of a KGB colonel fighting the Cold War in his own way was irresistible and the world's press rushed to the university winter stadium where the events were held.

Boris was upset but so too was Fox. The two had competed together for a decade, Fox said, and while they weren't bosom pals, "we'd often drunk vodka together in the evenings at various competitions, so there was a relationship." Fox was so rattled that his fencing went to pot, although he swam better than he'd ever done next day. It took the cross-country run, after which 36-year-old Fox needed oxygen, to be sure that Britain beat Czechoslovakia for the gold medal.

Onishchenko was reported to have been banned for life. Fox, on the other hand, had his own punishment: he developed Parkinson's disease.

23

How To Take A Bite At Success

Harry Mallin was a London policeman. He knew a crooked move when he saw it—or at any rate felt it—and part way through the boxing in Paris in 1924 he complained that he'd been bitten. Not by a bee but by his opponent, the Frenchman, Roger Brousse.

The French are noted gourmets but cannibalism isn't widespread and the Belgian referee took no notice. Or perhaps didn't understand him.

Brousse won the bout and Mallin, a good sport who accepted the referee's decision however wrong, shrugged his shoulders and left the ring. Disappointed, of course, because he was the defending champion from the previous Games, in Antwerp, and because he had never been beaten in more than 300 fights.

Mallin, like any good policeman, could show the evidence, though. Namely, a bright red bite mark on his chest that stayed there for a month.

"I was punishing him with my left hand when in the second round he came inside and I felt his teeth on my arm," Mallin recalled. "I pulled my arm away before I was bitten. But I wasn't so lucky in the next round. As he hung on, he fastened his teeth in my chest and threw a vicious right at my chin.

"At the final bell, I thought I had won well. But I was taking no chances and at the end I went over to the referee, who was making out his scorecard, and through an interpreter told him I had been fouled."

Well, evidence isn't always enough. A doctor looked at the red mark and then at Brousse. And he couldn't see how Brousse could have done it, given that he had a gum shield over his lower teeth. And the judges gave the Frenchman the fight, Mallin's first defeat in 14 years.

84   *Les Woodland*

The British boxing people refused to protest. It would be unsporting to challenge the referee, they said. But a Swedish official, Oscar Soderlund, said if the British wouldn't moan then he would. The appeal jury began sitting at 11:30 AM, knocked off for the afternoon and met again in the evening. By then they had further evidence, because an Argentinean boxer, Manuel Gallardo, said Brousse had tried to take a lump out of him as well. Brousse, on the other hand, said he had a habit of snapping his jaw when he threw a punch and Mallin had bumped his chest against his mouth.

By now word had spread and all the boxers taking part went on strike, except of course for the French who were defending one of their own in front of a home crowd. The boxing restarted an hour late only after the jury gave the decision to Mallin. That didn't persuade Brousse's supporters, though, and they put their man on their shoulders and, fighting off policemen, tried to put him in the ring where Mallin was about to start his next bout, the semifinal.

They were already furious because another Frenchman, Daniel Daney, lost his round even though he had obviously outboxed his Belgian opponent, Jo Beecken. They were so cross that they attacked Mallin's helpers in a subterranean alley leading to the dressing rooms on the other side of the Vel' d'Hiv cycling track. Mallin was there but helpers pushed him to one side while they sorted out the flurry of fists.

Mallin won the gold medal, the first boxer to successfully defend his Olympic title, and another Londoner, Jack Elliott, came second. Their bout was extensively booed by French fans, who by now had read in the morning papers of their man's disqualification. Mallin returned to England, his record intact, and retired, although he managed the British team at Berlin and Helsinki. He died in November 1969.

• • •

Skinny little Thomas Hamilton-Brown was thrown out after the first round of the boxing at the Berlin Games of 1936. He wasn't happy, sure that he had won, and took solace in food. He went on an eating binge.

The tiny South African was still metaphorically wiping his chops when the judges realized they'd made a mistake. They'd counted the points wrongly. He had won after all and he could go on to the second round. The problem was that there was nothing to him. He was just a lightweight and he'd put on two kilos. He tried sweating it off but when he went to the weigh-in for the next round, he was thrown out again for being too heavy.

Les Woodland

24

How To Have A Good Sulk

Dong-kih Choh wasn't sure he should have been disqualified. Let's not beat about the bush: he was hopping mad he'd been disqualified. So much so that this mouse-sized flyweight pulled his stool into the center of the ring, sat on it and refused to leave for 51 minutes.

That was the 1964 Games in Tokyo.

It set an example back in South Korea because in 1988 it happened all over again. This time it was a bantamweight rather than a flyweight but Byun Jong-il was just as cross. His trainers were even angrier and they attacked the referee as Jong-il went on strike on the canvas. And there he stayed, outdoing Dong-kih Choh by staying there for 67 minutes.

The row was over whether he'd butted his opponent. He, of course, thought not. The referee, a New Zealander called Keith Walker, docked him two points nevertheless. The boxer's coach, an assistant and as many fans as could climb into the ring mobbed Walker and began roughing him up. The rumpus ended after a while but Byun refused to budge. The only way to get him out of the ring was to turn off the stadium lights.

It was more than Walker could stand, especially after he'd needed an escort to get out of the stadium, and he flew home early. The president of the South Korean Olympic committee, Kim Chong-Ha, sympathized. He took full responsibility and resigned. Byun on the other hand turned professional and in 1993 became World Boxing Association champion.

It's difficult to avoid thinking there was something odd about South Korean boxing because a separate sensation happened at the same Games with a boxer of the same nationality.

Park Si-Hun was the home favorite against an American, Roy Jones, who was clearly better. The only medal he lacked in his career was the Olympic gold and he was well aware that he'd need more than his fists to get one at Seoul. He had to brave the judges as well.

Jones set out to make an immediate impression. He waded in like a combine harvester, flailing his opponent, all but skinning him. He "demolished" him, according to one reporter. He landed 86 blows to his opponent's 32 and stunned him into a standing eight-second count. And who won? The judges from Uganda, Uruguay and Morocco gave it to Park Si-Hun. The Russian and Hungarian judges favored Jones but they were outnumbered

Park Si-Hun kept his medal. To be fair, he was sporting about it. He lifted Jones' arm to encourage the crowd to cheer. Word has it he told Jones the judges had made the wrong decision. But he couldn't object to his own success and when Jones appealed he got nowhere.

Les Woodland

Five Things You Didn't Know You Didn't Know... About Boxing

1. Melagomas, from Caria in Asia Minor, used to win bouts despite never throwing a punch. He would engage opponents in a philosophical debate and explain that "to hit, to wound and be wounded was not bravery." His opponent would feel so ashamed that honor obliged him to leave the ring.

2. The only foreign boxer to win a medal at the London Games of 1908 was an Australian, Reg "Snowy" Baker. He thought he should have won the gold rather than the silver against the local man, John Douglas, and protested that the referee hadn't been impartial. Which he may not have been. The referee was Douglas' father.

3. Oscar "Golden Boy" de la Hoya won the boxing in Barcelona in 1992 only to have muggers take his wallet. They gave it back when they learned who he was.

4. "Sugar" Ray Leonard, then a 20-year-old light welterweight, pinned pictures of his girlfriend and their son to his socks before he beat the Cuban, Andres Aldama, to the gold medal in Montreal in 1976.

5. Seoul used two rings at the same time. One had a buzzer and the other a bell. All very well provided you remembered which was which. The bell went in a light-welterweight fight between Todd Foster of the USA and the Korean Chun Jin-chul. The Korean heard it and stopped but Foster, who was waiting for the buzzer, didn't. Neither the opportunity nor the target could be missed. Foster walloped the Korean on the eye.

25

How To See Truth In The Darkness

Very few of the people who ran the Nazi party lived to old age. The woman who courted controversy by filming the swastika Olympics, however, died when she was 101.

Leni Riefenstahl made the world's extravagant Games film in Berlin in 1936, using 30 cameramen and 300,000 meters of film. Or, if you're not too hot on metric measurements, around 18 miles of it. Three-fourths of it was unusable but what was left turned *Olympiche Spielen 1936* into an epic not of just sports reporting but cinema generally.

Guy Lapébie wasn't too concerned that it had been accused of lauding National Socialism. The war hadn't yet started, France hadn't yet been occupied, and he was happy to go and watch it. Not least because he had won a silver medal in the cycling. And he wanted to see what Riefenstahl had snapped of him.

He sat through film of divers and runners and then, suddenly, there he was whizzing along the Avus car circuit on the edge of Berlin. It had been an easy race with no hills and the distance, 100 kilometers, hadn't been enough to split the field. The medals would go to whoever could sprint fastest in the last few hundred meters.

Lapébie was an experienced rider—both he and his elder brother, Roger, went on to ride the Tour de France—and he had spotted the way the race would evolve. He'd edged close to the front to be ready for the dash to the line. He snicked into a higher gear, got out of the saddle, accelerated as hard as he could, got back into the saddle and kept up his speed to the end. He was certain to win. Except that suddenly he slowed down. He lost the gold medal to another Frenchman, Robert Charpentier, by the length of a bike.

One of the reasons Lapébie fancied watching the film was to see what had happened. He had ridden many sprints in his life and something

Les Woodland

of the sort had never happened before. And that was when he found out. Because there, on the huge screen, he saw an arm reach out, grab his shorts and give him a good tug backwards. Worse, the treacherous cheat was none other than Charpentier, his own teammate.

Well, Charpentier was a man politely described as "immensely self-confident." In other words, he was arrogant and boastful. The least competition was important to him. Even when he trained with friends, he'd brag: "I'm going to break away at kilometer 85: follow me if you can." A man like that couldn't tolerate being beaten for an Olympic title, not by such a small margin, still less by a teammate he didn't especially like.

Journalists watching the race had told Lapébie that something odd had taken place but, in the fraction of a second that it took, nobody could detect just what. Now Lapébie knew.

"From the day I saw that film, I considered myself the moral victor of the Olympic Games," he said. Which, Lapébie being politer than Charpentier, meant "Charpentier is a dirty cheat."

You won't be surprised that Charpentier didn't take that easily. "That's the biggest lie I've ever heard," he ranted. "I'll sue Lapébie for defamation even if it costs me a month's wages!"

It entertained journalists for ages, battle joined not only by the riders but their followers, their fans and, inevitably, a lot of people who knew nothing about it but thought they ought to join in. Charpentier and Lapébie realized in the end that they were prepared to snort and paw the ground but neither was prepared to go further. Lapébie took the diplomatic step of lying. He told *Miroir des Sports* that he'd been misquoted. What he'd said was that he had been tugged. He had never, of course, said that Charpentier did it.

No, of course he didn't.

26

How To Kill A Legend

Wa-tho-huck ("Bright Path"), an American Indian better known as Jim Frances Thorpe, became the only man to win both the decathlon and pentathlon in one year. He was then stripped of his victories, his medals were sent back, and his name was expunged from the records. He became one of America's star baseball players but died bankrupt in 1953.

Thorpe was born into the Thunder Clan of the Sac and Fox tribe around 22 May 1887 (the date is uncertain) on the reservation in Prague, Oklahoma. He attended Carlisle School, a government center for Indians, where he came under the wing of an American-football coach called Glenn "Pop" Warner.

Warner spotted Thorpe's talent and included him in a team that beat Harvard in a game in which Thorpe scored all the points. There seemed no limit to what Thorpe could do and in 1912 he was selected for Stockholm, where he came fourth in the high jump and seventh in the long jump. More significant, he won the old-style pentathlon by a record margin and the decathlon by 600 points. The double had never been achieved.

King Gustav of Sweden reportedly told him: "Sir, you are the greatest athlete in the world." Czar Nicolas of Russia gave him a jewel-encrusted chalice.

Thorpe returned to America with a ticker tape welcome on Broadway. Six months later his local paper reported that he had spent two college vacations playing summer baseball with the Rocky Mount Club in the Eastern Carolina Leagues. The money involved was small—£25 a week—but the American Olympic committee was appalled and declared him a professional. It took back his medals and returned his trophies to Stockholm. His triumphs were expunged from their books.

Les Woodland

Thorpe was forced into the professional sport that the AOC disliked and he signed a $5,000 contract to play baseball for New York Giants. By the end of his playing days in 1928, with the Chicago Cardinals, he had become an athletic institution. But there was little left for him when his sports days were over and he worked as a stunt man in films and, in 1949, as a bouncer. He became a drifter and an alcoholic. In 1951, with lip cancer, he was a case in the charity ward of a Philadelphia hospital.

His wife, Patricia, said: "We're broke. Jim has nothing but his name and his memories. He has spent money on his own people and has given it away. He has often been exploited."

Thorpe died of a heart attack on March 28, 1953, in Carlisle, Pennsylvania, still without his medals, which were returned posthumously only on October 13, 1982. Patricia Thorpe found that Oklahoma, where he had been born, was not interested in what she considered a suitable memorial. She read, though, that people in the towns of East Mauch Chunk and Mauch Chunk (the richest town in America during the 1800s, with more than 50 residents worth $1 million in modern values), Pennsylvania, had been motivated by the editor of their local paper to give a nickel a week to a development fund for the area.

Impressed by the community spirit, she went there and asked for help. Local leaders saw a chance to end the rivalry between the two towns and to create an inspiring image for their residents. In two polls, the towns agreed to change their name to Jim Thorpe.

Thorpe's memorial, on Route 903 northeast of the town, is a large granite block set in preserved land.

Five Curious Happenings That Don't Fit Anywhere Else

1. Bertil Sandström came second for Sweden in the equestrian dressage in 1936. But he was demoted to last for clicking to his horse. Apparently you're not allowed to click to your horse. Sandström said he had a creaking saddle but the judges didn't believe him.

2. A London enthusiast, Eddie Wingrave, volunteered to officiate at cycling events in London in 1948 to save the price of a ticket. The cost of volunteering was to buy his own blazer and tie. They came to more than the season ticket he'd been trying to avoid.

3. The German star, Toni Merkens, fouled his Dutch rival, Arie van Vliet, in the cycling sprint final in 1936. The crowd expected disqualification. Instead, Merkens was fined 100 Reichsmarks and allowed to keep the gold medal. The 1936 Games were in Berlin.

4. It took 10 years but the Chinese gymnast Dong Fangxiao finally had her bronze medal taken away. It turned out that she had been only 14 in 2000, two years younger than allowed.

5. It's become common for athletes to take drugs. But for the Irish show jumper, Cian O'Connor, it was the horse. But that wasn't all. O'Connor asked for a second test but the sample was stolen before it reached the laboratory. Someone broke into the Irish equestrian federation's offices and stole documents about one of O'Connor's other horses. Not until the spring of 2005 was O'Connor stripped of the gold medal he'd won the previous year.

27

How To Bring Sun To The Snow

Jamaica isn't the first place you'd go for snow but in 1988 the Caribbean island fielded a team for the bobsleigh in Calgary.

The dreamers were two Americans, George Fitch and William Maloney. Both lived in Jamaica and, for fun, went to watch a pushcart derby in Kingston. One said that it didn't look that different from bobsledding, not if you ignored the tropical heat and the absence of snow. You needed a good sprint to get going and if anywhere was known for sprinters, it was Jamaica.

They took their idea to the island's Olympic association. It was keen but other Jamaicans weren't. They turned up to a talk and a film but saw so many horrific crashes that most walked out before the lights came back on. So, if volunteers wouldn't do it, perhaps the army could. And it did, putting up Dudley Stokes, Devon Harris and Michael White. Others came, some stayed, some went but there was now a team.

By now the tourist board could see the publicity. It put up money and the team left to train in Lake Placid, New York. Their equipment was as poor as their technique and they crashed repeatedly. They got the cold shoulder from the international bobsleigh federation, reluctant to see its sport ridiculed. But, whether they liked it or not, the administrators shrugged when Jamaica entered a two-man and a four-man bob for the Games in Calgary.

The press coverage they got was bewildering. These were professional soldiers but in the public mind they had become pot-smoking dreadlocked Rastas keen on reggae. The image was helped by the team's spokesman, who was indeed bearded and a reggae singer. The team was besieged by journalists and fans. They were never going to win, of course. The two-man team came 35th but, for a nation where most people had never seen snow, still less raced in it, it was quite something.

Then the tale became still more lightheaded when the team looked for a replacement for one of its pushers—the people who get the bob started and then ride in the back—who'd been injured. The captain, Dudley Stokes, couldn't think of anyone but his brother. Chris was a good runner but he wasn't even at the Olympics and, more significantly, had never been in a bobsleigh. But he'd have a go, bro'.

Things went wrong. The push bar jammed on the first run for the two brothers and their teammates in the four-man race and then one of the team didn't jump aboard properly in the second. Dudley Stokes injured himself before the next run and the national coach went home. And then the whole thing crashed, literally, at 85 mph and the driver's head was pinned against the snow wall as the sleigh careered downhill out of control.

It had been fun while it lasted.

Les Woodland

28

How To Leave Blood On The Ice

It wouldn't, you'd think, be easy to go the wrong way in speed skating. If you set off in the right direction, you get back to where you started. But it's not as easy as that. Why? Because it's further for the skater on the outside and so the two skaters change sides every so often.

That was where the Dutchman, Sven Kramer, went wrong. He was leading in Vancouver in 2010 when his coach told him to move to the inside lane part way through the 10-kilometer. He should have been on the outside. He lost his gold medal, almost guaranteed him because he'd already won the Olympics twice and broken the Games record.

He'd won the 5-kilometer but, denied controversy on the ice, he courted it afterwards. An American TV reporter hurried along with a camera, pointed it at him and asked him to say who he was and what he'd won. The reporter wanted Kramer to identify himself for the sake of those compiling reports back in the studio. Kramer, though, took it as disrespect, that she hadn't even been watching.

"Are you stupid?" he asked in English, amazed. "Hell, no, I'm not going to do that."

Sound and vision were already running and Kramer's outburst became an internet hit. His reaction was a theme for an interview for Dutch television. He explained: "Come on, this is *belachelijk*. You've just become Olympic gold medal winner. She was there when it happened and then you have to sum up your whole biography. She's crazy."

Some sympathized but many laughed. What became clear was that Kramer wasn't used to not being recognized. He was one of his country's most famous athletes. Speed-skating is big in Holland. But Holland is small in the world.

His problems in the 10-kilometer came when his coach, Gerard Kemkers, shouted for him to change lane on the 17th lap, after 6,600 meters.

"I did what he said," Kramer sobbed afterwards, "but from the way the crowd reacted I knew something was wrong." He crossed the line in his orange skin suit, took off his goggles and believed he'd won. Then he got the news. Kemkers was even more distraught. It had happened in a fraction of a second while he was busy with his stopwatch, he said.

"My whole world fell in."

Kramer called him an idiot but felt more diplomatic in the morning. "The last few years have been too good to me to drop someone just like that," he said. "Our conversation wasn't easy but we parted as friends. And that's the most important. I'm not someone who stays angry for long. It happened. It's over."

Was it karmic revenge for calling the TV reporter an idiot? Or was the idiot Kemkers for shouting the wrong advice? Or was it Kramer, one of the world's most experienced skaters, for following it?

For you to decide.

Les Woodland

29

How To Put Beans Into The Games

The Games in 1932 were in Los Angeles. The world was in depression and countless people had lost all they had in the American stock market crash. And yet more than a million and a quarter people watched and the city made a profit of almost $1 million.

But not everybody had money to go. Even the competitors. The organizers sent their invitations on embossed card. They added that they'd feed everybody, house them and take them to their stadiums. To do this, they built the first Olympic village. They even negotiated with shipping companies to bring athletes from Europe for $500, a third the normal rate.

The result was that 1,500 competitors from 34 nations traveled to Los Angeles, although that was well down from the 3,015 of the previous Games, in Amsterdam. China, for instance, sent a single sprinter to represent its population of 400 million. He and the others spent their Olympics in a village of Mexican-style cottages with $2 a day in pocket money. But not all had reached the city easily. Brazil, for instance, wanted to send a team of 69 but didn't have the money. The coffee market had suffered in the world depression. The price had fallen from $25 to $7 a pound.

Brazil's answer was to put its team in a ship along with 50,000 pounds of coffee and sell the beans in every port in which the ship stopped. And so, in time to reach the opening ceremony on July 30, 68 men and a 17-year-old swimmer, Maria Lenk, boarded the *Itaquice* to stirring music from the Marine band. Behind them, cranes loaded the coffee.

It was a bright idea but undercaffeinated. Not enough people wanted Brazilian coffee. Some bought a bit. Trinidad, the first stop, didn't want a single bean. By the Panama Canal, only 24 of the 69 athletes had collected enough money to pay the toll.

For some reason, the *Itaquice* had guns on its stern. Its captain argued that that made it a warship and entitled to free passage. It was a good try but he was turned back. The ship radioed the *Banco de Brasil* and a messenger was sent with cash. That got it through the canal but still the coffee wouldn't sell. And there was worse to come.

When the *Itaquice* finally reached Los Angeles, the USA pointed out that everyone on board had to pay $1 to land. But the money had been spent in Panama.

Another message was sent, this time to the Brazilian consul in San Francisco, then still a long journey to the north. He agreed to send a messenger with a bag of Brazilian cash but, before he got to the ship, Brazil devalued its currency and it now cost eight milreis to get each athlete ashore instead of three.

There was enough money for only 24. Selectors picked those they thought had the best chance and the rest went back to sea in the hope of selling coffee to ports further north. Coffee is a big feature now of American life and Seattle has made a name from it. But things were different in 1932 and nobody wanted to know. The missing 45 made it back to Los Angeles only after the Games had closed.

There would be a fairy tale finish had the 24 Brazilians who made it come back in glory. But they didn't. Brazil competed in athletics, swimming, water polo, rowing and shooting. Their best: sixth in the pole vault.

You think that's sad enough?

Well, all 45 cheered when they saw Sugarloaf mountain but they groaned when they heard there'd been a national revolution. They planned to leave Rio de Janeiro on a train for São Paulo. But the revolution had halted the railways. They could have stayed until life became clearer but they found a freighter and the offer of a free lift to São Sebâstio island, and from there a small boat to the city itself.

They hiked for eight hours through the mountains and spent the night in a deserted shack. Higher in the mountains next day, a truck driver gave them a lift to Cacapava, where they finally took a train to São Paulo. It was, it's true, delayed by fighting between the army and the rebels but it did get there. And Brazil's coffee Olympics were finally over.

Les Woodland

30

How To Nip Enthusiasm In The Budd

Few combinations were more likely to start a rumpus. She was white and from a country despised for its treatment of blacks. Her homeland was excluded from the Olympics. And she was paid to change her nationality by a British newspaper that once shouted "Hurrah for the Blackshirts."

Zola Budd was 5'2" and ran like the wind. Barefoot. She was also South African. The right-wing London *Daily Mail* paid her family £100,000 for her story and promised to push through her application for a British passport. She could then run for Britain in the Olympics on the grounds that her grandfather had been born in England.

"To the world," said the *New York Times,* "Budd was a remorseless symbol of South Africa's segregationist policies. To the *Daily Mail,* she was a circulation windfall."

Demonstrations met her in England. She was booed and insulted. It didn't help that the few words she managed were in a pronounced South African accent. How could this sales stunt for a right-wing newspaper be British? And how did she have the right to a passport so quickly when others had to wait years? And how come the *Daily Mail* had such sway with the government?

The Mail called her the "hottest property in world athletics."

"Property" wasn't the best chosen word.

The paper organized her press conference and played the theme from "Chariots of Fire". She qualified for the British team in her first race, 3,000-meter in 9 minutes 2.06 seconds.

Rows followed her everywhere. The mayor of Crawley, near London's second airport at Gatwick, canceled her invitation to run there rather than face "political connotations and antiapartheid demonstrators." She was banned from the Commonwealth Games.

"Until I got to London in 1984, I never knew Nelson Mandela existed," she said. "I was brought up ignorant of what was going on. All I knew was the white side expressed in South African newspapers—that if we had no apartheid, our whole economy would collapse."

In the end it was Mary Decker who collapsed. To Budd, she was a hero. Decker's picture was pinned to her bedroom wall in South Africa. The two were the target for reporters at the Olympics of 1984, Decker the glamor girl of the United States running in Los Angeles, and Budd the South African waif who'd changed nationality to escape a worldwide ban. Few reports noted that the favorite was actually Maricica Puica, the Romanian who'd run the fastest time of the year.

The first half of the race went well. But at 1,700 meters, Budd and Decker bumped but continued running. A couple of steps again and Decker caught Budd's right ankle with her spikes. Budd stumbled but Decker fell, clutching her right thigh. She was carried off the track in tears. Budd finished seventh, rattled, booed by the crowd, and Puica won. Decker had fallen in front of her home crowd; judges disqualified Budd but then changed their mind.

Budd apologized to Decker but, she said, the American snapped: "Don't bother!"

Decker said many years later: "Some people think she tripped me deliberately. I happen to know that wasn't the case at all. The reason I fell is because I am and was very inexperienced in running in a pack."

Budd won the world cross-country championship in 1985 and 1986, and the European 3,000-meter championship, and set a world record for 5,000 meters. But her best was past and in 1988, disillusioned, she went back to South Africa, never again to live in the country whose passport she had so controversially obtained. Now known as Zola Pieterse, a mother of three, she says of 1984: "It's like reading a novel about a totally different person. I think: 'That didn't happen to me?'"

• • •

In the 1912 marathon Kennedy McArthur and Charles Gitsan, South African teammates, were well ahead of the field. On the understanding

Les Woodland

that McArthur would wait for him, Gitsan stopped for a drink of water. McArthur ran on and won by a minute and two seconds.

• • •

Rhodesia (now Zimbabwe)—which happens to be South Africa's neighbor—is the only country to have offered to march behind a Boy Scout flag to avoid another apartheid ban in the Games. It was a flippant remark and did little to please officialdom but it provided an entertaining spat during September 1971.

In 1965 the country had declared itself independent of Britain, under its first native-born prime minister, Ian Smith. His words "the white man is the master of Rhodesia" haunted the nation's participation in the Olympics, especially as the country's politics were so close to those of the neighbors.

31

How To Be, Er, Not Quite
The Best Ever

There's a tradition that the man in charge of the Olympics worldwide—because it's never been a woman—praises each city at the closing ceremony for holding "the best Olympiad ever."

Such was the chaos that surrounded the 1996 Games in Atlanta that he limited himself to calling them the "most exceptional." He knew of which he spoke. The Games were criticized for the nightmare of Atlanta's transport, for its gross commercialism, and for the rickety computer links. In the midst of all this, a bomb went off. And yet, on the 100th year of the modern Olympics, it should have been all so different.

The London *Daily Mail* headlined "Olympic chaos". *France-Soir* observed: "Africa has been deprived of the Games since their creation with the pretext that African countries don't have the necessary infrastructure. After Atlanta, any country in the world can apply to host the Games."

Even the home side began pitching into its own goal. The *Los Angeles Times* spoke of "bum steers in bumfuzzled Atlanta."

What persuaded the IOC to give the Games to Atlanta was the city's light railway. It was the first thing they were shown. And impressive it is, to tell the truth. Atlanta has the USA's second largest airport and the city showed it could get athletes from there to their stadiums in 20 minutes. The railway could carry 2,000 people every two or three minutes. But even the railway bosses knew they couldn't carry the numbers who'd come for the Olympics and they kept telling the organizers so.

It took time to make the point that buses would be needed and that the rail company, which also operated the buses, would have none to spare. Atlanta already had its hands and buses full with everyday traffic. When the message sank in, the city looked elsewhere. George Turner, who ran the rail network, said Atlanta would need 1,167 buses. But the city opted for just 1,000. Even for those, they needed 3,000 drivers, mechanics and the rest.

The organizers thought, Turner said, that "people were going to come out and work for the Games just because it was the Olympics. I think they were initially offering drivers $6 an hour."

Volunteers and local drivers felt insulted and stayed away. The city recruited from elsewhere, inexperienced people who didn't know the buses and, even more, didn't know Atlanta. Joseph Hall of the *Toronto Star* wrote: "Press reports from the time bemoan long lineups, broken down vehicles, confusion and late or nonexistent buses delivering, or failing to deliver, spectators and reporters to their venues."

A French journalist wrote of petty restrictions. "The bus from the stadium went past our hotel. We asked the driver if she'd open the doors at the next traffic holdup and we'd step out. She said she wouldn't. When we asked why, she said her instructions were to drive to the depot without stopping. We pointed out that she was stopping all the time, in the traffic. She still refused.

"Eventually one of us pointed to the sign banning smoking on the bus. He asked what would happen if he lit a cigarette. She said her orders were to stop the bus and demand he get off. So he lit a cigarette and we all got off."

A spectator wrote on his blog: "On my first night at the Olympics, the bus driver taking me and about 35 other people back to our cars got lost. Our half-hour trip took 1½ hours. On my second night, another bus driver prepared to get on the wrong highway until a chorus of Atlanta natives on the bus yelled in unison, directing him to the correct road.

"Last night, on my way to the Olympics, our bus took the side view mirror off a merging Jeep. We pulled over to the side of the road and sat for a half-hour while police filled out their reports. Then, when we got on the bus to head back, an Olympics representative got on the bus and publicly asked if there was anyone who could give our driver directions on how to get to the drop-off point."

There was worldwide criticism of commercialism. Atlanta is the home town of Coca-Cola and it more than showed. On top of that, Atlanta competed with the IOC for advertising and sponsorship. The organizers said heavy commercial sponsorship was part of American capitalism.

Samaranch said "Well, done Atlanta" in his closing speech but left out the "best ever" he had used after all his other Games. The accolade returned for the next Games, in Sydney.

Les Woodland

32

How To Be A Tumblin' Sno-Muffin

The point about being a snow muffin is to look cool. Leave it to the downhill skiers to be sleek and the cross-country brigade to gasp in agony. If you can't be cool at snow boarding, why bother? Dress like an orphan and act like an adolescent. And show off without ever admitting it.

That seemed the ambition of the American, Lindsey Jacobellis, in 2006. Anyone else would have just pressed for the line. She had a whacking lead and was guaranteed the gold medal if she kept her head. But she didn't. The final jump came and rather than tackling it like an expert, she showed off and dropped like a novice. She tried to grab her board as she sailed off the jump. But she failed and plunged to the snow. She was still lying there, getting her breath back and perhaps reflecting on the cost of cool, when Tanjan Frieden whizzed by and won.

"I was having fun," Jacobellis said. "Snow boarding is fun." Vainly she tried to explain that she'd been keeping the board still. Later she admitted she had just been larking about.

A year later, in the X Games—a commercial tournament of so-called "extreme" sports organized by an American TV company—she did it again. She fell over while in the lead. She did win that competition the following year but Tumblin' Lindsey was back in form—or out of form—for the Olympics of 2010. She got as far as the semifinal and fell over again. She landed badly after a jump, nearly slithered into another competitor, tried to stop herself and skidded through a gate. That was enough for instant disqualification but not enough for Jacobellis: she went further and slid right off the course.

"Thus did she pass into legend," one commentator observed, "Lindsey Jacobellis, symbol of foolish pride, poster girl for hot-dogging."

It didn't prevent her selling her name for corn flakes commercials and to sell credit cards.

Les Woodland

33

How To Be A Sexy Beach Babe

Ethelda Bleibtrey was the USA's first female Olympic swimming champion and the only person to win all the women's swimming events at any Games. She is also the only Olympic athlete to have been charged with public indecency for removing her socks.

Bleibtrey won three gold medals at Antwerp in 1920 and says only fate kept her from four. "I was the world record holder in backstroke but they didn't have women's backstroke, only freestyle, in those Olympics."

Prudish American society insisted that women wore all-over costumes on the beach. New York's law insisted they could not bare "their lower extremities." So when Bleibtrey removed her stockings on a Manhattan beach in 1919, she was jailed for public nudity. Only public anger over her arrest changed the law.

She was arrested again in 1928 when the *New York Daily News* got her to dive into the Central Park reservoir in New York in a campaign to open it for public swimming. The paper tipped off the police, for which arrest Bleibtrey was paid $1,000, but spent a night in jail. The stunt worked because it embarrassed the mayor, Jimmy Walker, and he gave New York its first big swimming pool in Central Park. It worked for Bleibtrey, too, because she needed the money to pay debts. A planned theater tour turned to disaster when the tank in which she was to swim leaked and flooded the stage.

Bleibtrey began swimming to recover from polio. She turned professional in 1925 and died in Florida in 1978.

34

How To Go Out With A Bang

The American pistol shooter James Howard Snook made headlines for more than his gold medal at Antwerp in 1920. He murdered his mistress with a hammer and was executed after a trial so spiced with sex and drugs that nobody dared publish all. He lies now in a disguised grave.

Snook was a balding professor of animal medicine at Ohio State university, where he began a three-year affair with a student who worked there, Theora Hix. He was 48 and married. His wife, Helen, said she knew nothing of the affair and she defended him throughout the trial, which took place in the summer of 1929.

Snook may have been good with animals, and his wife obviously loved him, but he lacked the knack with Theora. She said she knew more about sex than he did and suggested he'd better "read up", as he put it. She suggested books such as *The Art of Love*, and he read them. He obviously learned, too, because his court evidence was so sexually explicit that local newspapers were too terrified to print it. The court's shorthand-taker, though, delighted the nation with his uncensored account—until, at any rate, the police confiscated it.

The account detailed how Hix introduced Snook to oral sex and took cannabis, Spanish fly and cocaine. Snook got her drugs from the university pharmacy and took some himself. They met in a boarding house for sex and drugs. But Hix had a younger lover, Marion Meyers, and repeatedly told Snook he was a better lover and more generously endowed.

It was Meyers the police picked up when two teenagers found Hix beaten and slashed at the range where Snook had been teaching her to shoot. But Meyers could prove his affair with Hix had been over for a year. The police then turned to Snook, questioned him for 19 hours with few breaks and beat him into confessing. There was blood on his clothes and car, and he had a hammer and a knife stained with Hix's blood.

The trial lasted less than 30 days, packed with details. People queued from the early hours to watch. Snook said Hix was unsatisfied by "conventional sex." Their three-year affair became increasingly voracious. She demanded sex somewhere secluded, "where I can scream." Snook drove her to the rifle range.

"She grabbed open my trousers and went down on me then, and she didn't do it very nicely and she bit me and got hold of my privates and pulled so hard I simply could not stand it. I got hold of something and hit her with it. I finally got her loose, very nearly twisted her arm off and she sat up there a little bit and said, 'Damn you, I will kill you, too.'

"I hit her once then, I hit her again and she slid right out on the ground and I followed her out. I got up behind her and hit her once more with the hammer and she went down and her head hit against the running board."

Verdict: guilty. Sentence: death. Outcome: a nation titillated by drugs and oral sex. Snook was executed in the electric chair at Ohio Penitentiary on February 28, 1930. He is buried in lot 243 of section 87 of Green Lawn Cemetery. His tombstone says only "James Howard". Such was the sensation that his last name was omitted so the grave would not be vandalized.

35

How To Be An Oddjob Man

Nobody outside his homeland had heard of Harold Sakata when he arrived to lift weights for America in the London Olympics of 1948. But by the time he died in 1982, he was one of the best known people in the world—although not by his own name. Because Sakata became famous as the bowler-hatted killer, Oddjob, who protected Goldfinger in the James Bond film.

Born Toshiyuki Sakata near Holualoa, Hawaii, on January 7, 1920, one of six brothers and four sisters, Sakata was a tribute to advertisements of the "You too can have a body like mine" type that were popular between the wars. Pictures of muscular men in magazines when he was 18 made him embarrassed of being just 1 meter 72 (5'8") and 51 kilograms (112 pounds). He took up weightlifting at the island's YMCA for Asians. A year of training made him 10kg heavier and he began entering lifting contests.

He moved to the American mainland and began calling himself Harold. He came second in the US weightlifting championship in 1948 and was picked for that year's Olympics, going there with his teammate, Stan Stanczyk. He won the silver medal.

By now Sakata had a 51-centimeter (20-inch) neck and a 127-centimeter (50-inch) chest. He became Mr. Waikiki in 1949 and gave up weightlifting for professional wrestling. He was billed as "Mr. Sakata, the Human Tank" and, in Australia, as "Tosh Togo." He swallowed his pride by explaining: "I couldn't eat my trophies."

A TV appearance in London as Tosh Togo attracted the filmmakers Harry Saltzman and Albert Broccoli, who contracted him to play Oddjob in "Goldfinger", which they filmed in 1957 and 1958. They were taken by his build—he weighed 129kg (284 pounds)—and his intimidating stare. He had no acting experience but he wouldn't have

Les Woodland

any lines as an expressionless bodyguard, called Oddjob because, Auric Goldfinger says in the film: "That describes his functions on my staff."

His deadly weapon was an alloy-rimmed bowler hat. It took him five months to master spinning it. He told the *Star-Bulletin* in December 1965: "I worked with a plaster statue of a girl and aimed for the neck. I got so I could topple the head off every time. It made me very conscious of necks." He took to wearing the hat permanently but eventually sold it. In September 1998 Christie's auctioned it to an anonymous buyer for £61,750.

Pretty deadly, too, was his karate chop. Asked to put "more realism" into a fight, he reputedly put Sean Connery out of action for several days. He traded on the Oddjob image for the rest of his life. In TV commercials, for instance, he was so in pain from a sore throat that he smashed everything around him. Only the cough syrup he was advertising could, placate him.

Sakata died of liver cancer on July 29, 1982, aged 62.

36

How To Be An Amateur Spook

The world was a hot place in 1960. Not the summer, although in Rome that was warm enough, but in politics. The Italian organizers in 1960 were so concerned that cold war—or worse—would break out in the arena that diplomats paid tactful calls on governments around the world to ask that the Games were kept "free from activity of a political or propaganda nature."

Gabriele Paresce told the US State Department he had no worries about the USA, good gracious no. It was the communists who worried Italy. Politicians and sports officials were "seriously concerned that the Iron Curtain countries should be admonished not to exploit contacts at the Games for propaganda purposes." The message was: "No propaganda, or we throw you out!"

The State Department—in charge of American foreign relations—said it had no control over sport but that it would pass on the message. The American team was at that moment in New York before flying to Rome. Its press director, Arthur Lentz, promised America would behave. The very next day—Saturday, August 13—the CIA called one of the sprinters, who was in bed at the Vanderbilt Hotel in Manhattan and feeling unwell. He would much rather have been training with the rest of the team at Van Cortlandt Stadium, in the Bronx.

"Is this David Sime?" the voice asked. He knew enough to pronounce the name *Simm*. "Can we talk?"

"About what?"

The caller wouldn't say but explained that he was speaking for the government, which needed his help. Sime was understandably intrigued. He sat in his room as the agent said the CIA had been watching Soviet runners who'd been at a track competition between the USA and USSR. Reports from behind the Iron Curtain suggested one in particular could be interested in defecting.

Sime didn't believe him. He was sure his pals at the training ground had set him up. But the man was insistent. He pulled his government identification from his pocket and said: "We'd like you to come to Washington. We'll have you back tonight."

They flew to Washington. A black car took them to a nondescript building and a secure room. One of the three in the room said: "Here's the guy's name" and they showed him a picture of Igor Ter-Ovanesyan, a long-jumper.

Igor Aramovich Ter-Ovanesyan was a star on the rise. He won medals in the Olympics and in European championships. Why he had aroused the CIA's interest never became clear. He may have considered defecting but he stayed in Russia even after the fall of communism and became the national coach.

For his part, Sime was probably chosen because he had coached in Burma while the USA and the Soviet Union conducted a hidden battle to control the country and entice its athletes. Sime may not have had much knowledge of Russian athletes but he knew more than most about athletics as world politics. He could see, for instance, that both the USA and the USSR were trying to recruit Burmese runners. The two nations' contingents were in all but neighboring rooms.

Sime agreed to play the spook. He went to Rome and contacted Ter-Ovanesyan. They got on well and had dinner several times. They could exchange experiences, even with a language problem. They got on so well that Sime introduced Ter-Ovanesyan to his wife. Things went far enough that the question of defecting could come up. Ter-Ovanesyan was interested and Sime told him what he knew.

That was the signal for the CIA man to join them. He spoke in Armenian, Ter-Ovanesyan's native language. And he urged his man too much. Ter-Ovanesyan backed off, killing the conversation. He didn't trust that the man wasn't a KGB man.

"The CIA screwed it up," Sime said. "They scared him."

The spooks didn't give up, though. They asked Sime to try again a few years later.

"I said hi to him from 20 feet away," Sime said. "He saw me, smiled and said, 'David, it's so good to see you. I'd love to talk to you, but I can't.' And he turned his back and walked away."

The Olympics' 50 Craziest Stories

How Not To Go Home And How To Stay Away

The first person to defect during an Olympics was an official rather than a competitor. Marie Provaznikova was head of the technical commission for women's gymnastics and director of the winning Czech team. She refused to return to Czechoslovakia after the Games in 1948.

The London *Guardian* reported on August 19: "Mrs Marie Provaznikova (57), leader of the Czech women's athletic contingent at the Olympic Games, who has obtained permission from the Prague authorities to go to the United States for a year as a gymnastic instructor, stated last night that she did not intend to return to Czechoslovakia.

"'I am a political refugee and proud of it,' she told a reporter. 'When I left Czechoslovakia I did not intend to return, although no one else knew that. I am a member of the Beneš party.'

"She said she was afraid that if she went back she would have to countenance the removal of some of her friends from the Sokol movement (the Czech national fitness movement, of which she is a prominent leader). 'There is no freedom in Czechoslovakia now—no freedom of speech, or of the press, or of assembly.'"

She went to America, stayed there, became a professor, and died aged 101 in 1992.

The Russians, on the other hand, tried to break *into* the Games. They hadn't entered—largely because they hadn't joined the international Olympic movement—but nevertheless planned to send wrestling, boxing, swimming, basketball and gymnastics teams once the Olympics had started. The note from the British Foreign Office told its men in Moscow to explain that the idea was "impractical" because events were already advanced.

Japan's entry in 1948 was rejected because of "serious public resentment." And the Japanese were still "technically enemies" because peace had yet to be signed.

The Foreign Office internal memo from the Japan Department said: "Lord Burghley [the former international runner in charge of the London Olympics] pointed out that neither the Germans nor the Japanese had been thrown out of the International Olympic Committee because hitherto they had lain doggo and it was not thought desirable to raise the question which might cause unnecessary bother."

Germany saw how things were and hadn't even asked to join in.

"Lord Burghley... pointed out that it would be a quite impossible position if the Japanese came, for instance, they could not attend any official functions as they were still technically enemies and could certainly never be present at any function where The King was present."

The memo ended: "There might be a certain amount of publicity for our refusal to allow the Japanese to come and it might therefore be better for the reply to be carefully phrased."

• • •

The Russian invasion of Czechoslovakia sent the gymnast Vera Caslavska into hiding in Mexico. She had signed a petition demanding greater reform in her country. Only when she heard that Russian officials wouldn't grab and deport her did she win four gold and two silver medals.

✍

38

How To Leap Into The Arms Of God

Joe Faust couldn't see the bar and posts of the high jump without imagining a crucifix. In the moments before he started his run to straddle the bar in the old-fashioned way, he promised himself he was leaping into the arms of God. He was, you have guessed, religious.

This young American had trained for seven years before the Olympics in Rome, at first not getting much higher than three feet. His coach, though, saw potential and promised he had the talent to reach the national team. It took time but he was right.

Faust went to Rome, loved the atmosphere and the old buildings and, above all, adored seeing the Pope. At the gates of the stadium he met a penniless Swede who had lost his money; he played the Good Samaritan and took him to eat in the competitors' canteen.

But heaven was looking elsewhere. In a sport in which Dick Fosbury popularized the Fosbury Flop, Faust just flopped. He survived the morning heats and went into the afternoon with the other 16 who hadn't been eliminated. He looked again at the crucifix and trusted God would take care of his bad back. The effort of leaping was penance for his sins and a safe landing was God's sign. But today it didn't happen.

He got up and he got down but he rose just 6'4¾". For a man who had jumped four inches higher at 15, and seven feet when he was 17, it was a disaster. Still more embarrassing, he and the other qualifiers had already beaten at least 6'6¾" that morning. He walked off and didn't jump again. He finished 17th, worst of the qualifiers. His career was over.

He went back to California, still 17 and the youngest of the American athletics team, changed his name to Zachary and fasted for three days outside the New Clairvaux abbey. He pondered God's purpose for

118   *Les Woodland*

individual molecules way beneath the earth and, more practically, he thought of the woman with whom he had fallen in love. Unable to answer the molecule question and unable to resist the woman, he gave up becoming a monk, married, had children, got divorced, and went back to pondering molecules.

Last heard of, 50 years after falling short of heaven in Rome, he was living in a single room on a hillside in California, surrounded by religious books. Outside he had made a makeshift frame and crossbar and the track of worn soil that led to it showed he was still jumping. Up as his penance, down in retribution. But no nearer an Olympic medal.

The Olympics' 50 Craziest Stories

39

How To Fall Into The Arms Of Ignominy

Nobody has ever said that he died of drugs. The verdict was sunstroke and a fall. But the chairman of the Dutch cycling federation said "whole cart loads" of drugs were taken in the Rome Olympics—and he didn't say in cycling alone.

It was cycling, though, that brought the problem to the fore. It was the opening day and the 100-kilometer time-trial was going to take most of it. The race is the fastest that cycling has on the road. Teams of four set off at the same time and take turns creating a slipstream for each other before swinging to one side and dropping to the back of the line. It is an act of beautiful precision—but it does take precision. The slightest lapse and one rider will touch the back wheel only centimeters ahead and fall at 60 kilometers per hour or more.

Knud Jensen, one of the quarter from Denmark, began to lose that cohesion. He started riding erratically, then began weaving across the road. Teammates rode to each side to keep him upright. But then he came crashing down to the right of the road, landing heavily on his front although with his left shoulder touching the ground first. He died in hospital, aged 23.

Knud Enemark Jensen became a choice for the Olympics in 1959, when he won three races and finished in the first three of six more. He and his teammates came second in the team time-trial in the Nordic championships. That guaranteed his place in Rome.

Newspaper reports said the temperature on the opening day reached 42 Celsius (108 F). It troubled Jensen and, only slightly less, his teammate Jorgen Jorgensen. The four rode well despite that until they were 20 kilometers from the finish. There Jensen collapsed.

Les Woodland

A military ambulance took him and two other riders to the Sant Eugenio hospital in Rome, and there Jensen died later that day. A trainer for the team said he had given them Ronicol, a stimulant that also makes blood run more freely to the muscles. That is indeed what the three pathologists found in the autopsy. A separate report says they also found eight pills of phenylisopropylamine and 15 of amphetamine, and that he had drunk coffee. The coffee could have been incidental but there was a belief among athletes that it increased the efficiency of amphetamine.

This noticeably precise claim is made by the Italian researcher, Lorella Vittozzi, but doesn't appear in the final report. Instead, the autopsy surgeons say he died from the heat and not from the drugs. His family received one million lire in compensation.

Sixteen years later, Wlodzimierz Golebewski painted a clearer picture in his history of Olympic cycling. The vice-president of the International Amateur Cycling Federation said: "This young man had taken a large overdose of drugs, which had been the cause of his death. No one has ever proved whether he took the overdose himself or whether the drug was administered by someone else without his knowledge."

There had been drug-taking in many sports as far back as the 19th century, and Tom Hicks all but died after the marathon in 1904. Arnold Beckett, who became head of Olympic dope-testing, said: "Used ampoules and syringes were found in some changing rooms at the 1952 winter Olympics in Oslo." But doping was only just starting to cause alarm.

Jensen's death served to force the hand of sports administrators. Pierre Dumas had been shocked by drug-taking in the Tour de France since he joined it as its doctor in 1952. He was powerless to do anything, though, because cycling like other sports had no rules to stop it.

Dumas used Jensen as a lever to force the international cycling union to test riders in the 100-kilometer at the next Games, in Tokyo. And that experience led doctors to report to the IOC president, Avery Brundage, what they had done and the results they'd had.

Tests began in 1968. Which wasn't too soon. The American hammer thrower, Harold Connolly, told a Senate committee: "I knew of any number of athletes in the 1969 Olympic team who had so much scar tissue and so many puncture holes on their backsides that it was difficult to find a fresh spot to give them a new shot. The overwhelming majority of the international track and field athletes I know would take anything and do anything short of killing themselves to improve their athletic performance."

Documents opened in 1990 showed East Germany systematically used drugs on its athletes, including giving anabolic steroids to women, especially swimmers.

• • •

The first competitor to die during the Olympics was Francisco Lazaro of Portugal. He collapsed during the marathon in Stockholm in 1912 and died in hospital.

Les Woodland

40

How To Win A Gold Medal For Drains

It is safe to take a bet on town planning as an Olympic competition because nobody ever believes it to be true. Nevertheless medals were awarded for town planning and for the arts from 1908 to 1936, although formally only from Stockholm in 1912.

The job was always taken on by the IOC rather than the organizing town, which generally couldn't be bothered or couldn't manage it. Including the arts, including town planning, was de Coubertin's idea. But, said Henri Pouret, an expert on the subject: "Competitive art within the framework of the Olympics declined almost from its beginning, mainly because of the tremendous problems of transporting exhibits, mustering large orchestras to play new works and the fact that prospective competitors who already enjoyed a certain reputation preferred to be judges rather than to be judged."

The problem of transporting exhibits was never greater than in town planning and architecture, of course. You couldn't pack a new town hall or sewer system in a suitcase. And the competition inevitably favored the home town, since all judges had to do was walk down the street to have a look. The winner at Berlin in 1936 was the main stadium itself. The runner-up, the American Charles Downing, couldn't be as convincing with his plan for a marina park in Brooklyn.

An odd situation arose in the music competition. Pouret says: "From 1936 on, musical works were divided into works for orchestras, instrumental works and songs. The first prize for instrumental works was never awarded."

Frustratingly, he doesn't say why. Nor why not even the second prize was awarded in London in 1948, the highest place being only third. It is an odd place, the arts world.

In 1948 town planning was won by Yrjo Lindegren of Finland for his athletics center in Varkaus. In fact sports arenas took all three places, with Werner Schindler and Edy Knupfer coming second with a Swiss arena and Ilmari Niemelainen third with another stadium for Finland, although this time in Kemi.

Even de Coubertin once won a medal, although he disguised himself generously as George Hohorod *and* Martin Eschbach of *Germany*. Deceit alone should have won. He contributed a lengthy work called *Ode to Sport*, which he wrote in French but offered in German to keep up the pretense that he was two Germans at the same time.

Perhaps just the first verse suffices. It usually does:

"O Sport, delight of the Gods, distillation of life! In the gray dingle of modern existence, restless with barren toil, you suddenly appeared like the shining messenger of vanished ages, those ages when humanity could smile. And to the mountain tops came dawn's first glimmer, and sunbeams dappled the forest's gloomy floor."

And so it went on for eight more numbered verses. After 1948 the Olympics didn't bother again. That year did provide the Olympics' oldest winner, however. The British artist, John Copley, won a silver a month before his 74th birthday.

• • •

The Games held a competition in 1954 to find an anthem. The winner, Michael Spisiak of Poland, asked so much for it to be played that it's never been heard since 1956.

Les Woodland

41

How To Open The Games Yourself

Helsinki in 1952 was the Games so good they opened it twice. Or nearly, anyway. Finland was the smallest country and its capital the smallest city to have flown the Olympic rings. The world was getting back to normal after the war and the austerity of the previous Games in London had started to pass.

This was the spirit in which spectators and competitors gathered for the opening ceremony. Outside Scandinavia, Finland was unknown and anything could happen there, especially now that the opening ceremony was becoming more elaborate with each Olympiad.

"This explains," said Peter Wilson of the London *Daily Mirror*, "why a rather plump lady, partly veiled and wearing what appeared to be a flowing nightdress was able to get on the track, complete a half circuit of it, and actually ascend the official rostrum and begin a speech with what sounded something like 'Peace.'"

Astonished officials thought she was a part of the ceremony they had overlooked and nobody intervened. But her fatness proved her undoing. She was so out of breath from her wobble around the track that she could barely speak. She mumbled "Peace..." and the head organizer, Eric von Frenckell, acted where others dared not. He bundled her out of the way—a job completed by the police, who said she was Barbara Rotbraut-Pleyer, "a deranged German student" but known instantly to the papers because of her white outfit as the "Peace Angel."

She had come to address "Humanity", she explained when her breath returned and once the police let her. This so intrigued a reporter from a Sunday paper in Britain that he asked the police question after question. The police, not understanding or perhaps not caring, assumed he was an accomplice and arrested him as well.

Helsinki was embroiled in hot wars past and cold wars present. The city was to have run the 1940 Olympics instead of Tokyo, which had had them removed because of Japan's war with China. Then came the second world war and Helsinki's chance didn't come until 1952. By then a cold war had broken out between the European Communist bloc and the west.

The Soviet Union had never entered the Olympics but chose 1952 for its debut. It intended to use Finland for day trips, flying competitors in from Leningrad when they were needed and then out again afterwards. In the end, the IOC agreed to give it, Bulgaria, Czechoslovakia, Hungary, Poland, Romania and Yugoslavia a separate Olympic village.

This went against the Olympic spirit and, Peter Wilson wrote: "It is hard to understand how the International Olympic Committee, which had strained at so many gnats, allowed itself to swallow this particular camel. Probably they were anxious to accommodate the lost sheep which had returned."

There had been a long antagonism between Finland and the USSR and, before it, with Czarist Russia. Sweden gave Finland to Russia in 1809, having run it since 1155. It regained its independence in 1917, lost it again in a war with Russia in 1939, regained it with help from Germany in 1941 and was then again invaded by Russia in 1944. It took until 1955 to pay off the reparations that Moscow demanded. It also lost 12 per cent of its territory.

National identity was therefore more than usually important to Finland when the Games opened and Finnish joy was all the greater when its national hero, Paavo Nurmi, ran unexpectedly into the stadium to bring the Olympic torch. Nurmi had been retired for nearly 20 years and spectators wept to see him again. He could only have smiled, too, because years earlier he had been banned from the Olympics as a professional.

Nurmi was now 55 and had rheumatism but he ran smoothly with the torch, lit a candelabra at the side of the track, then handed the torch to Hannes Kohlemainen, winner of three gold medals in 1912, who climbed the steps to light the permanent flame.

Wilson recalled: "It was rumored at the time that the IOC had not altogether approved of the selection of Nurmi as a torchbearer.

Les Woodland

That was hardly surprising for the International Amateur Athletic Federation, the senior sports federation, had declared the Finn ineligible to compete in the 1932 Los Angeles Games—for alleged breaches of amateurism—where he might well have added top his total of medals. But anyone who knew the stern independence of the Finns would have known that it would take more than the unspoken veto by the IOC to make them abandon their hero."

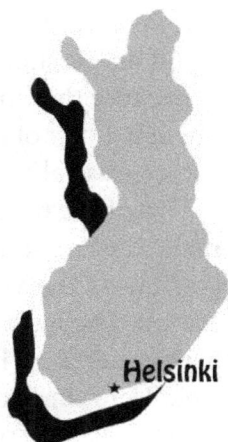

Helsinki

42

How To Light Your Own Light

The Peace Angel is not alone in hoaxing the Olympics. The mayor of Sydney, Pat Hills, was so keen to join in the Olympic spirit in 1956—when the Games were in the rival city of Melbourne—that he arranged to run part of the way with the Olympic torch. He stood ready to receive it and have his moment of glory. He bounced lightly on the spot in anticipation as the bearer approached. He put out his arm to receive it, ready to set off on his short run. But his grin turned to surprise. And then alarm. Because the "torch" he was handed was a chair leg, a plum-pudding can and a pair of burning army underpants.

The real flame's passage across Australia from Cairns to Melbourne also wasn't without incident. Drowning rain put it out and then, when the sun returned, the heat made the runners wilt. The man scheduled to carry it through Sydney as far as the waiting mayor was a cross-country champion, Harry Dillon. The mayor was to take it, say a few words, then pass it to another runner, Bert Button.

They say that 30,000 people were there to see it happen. A police escort formed around the runner as the crowd yelled its excitement. They could see the flame bobbing nearer. But then someone said "That's not the torch" and the mayor took a closer look, realized with all the experience that running an internationally famous city gives that this was a pair of kerosene-soaked underpants burning with a greasy flame and dropped it.

The man who had brought it vanished into the crowd. Only years later did it turn out that he was Barry Larkin, a student at St. Johns College. He and eight others were protesting, he said, at the reverence given to a tradition founded in Nazi Germany. In fact he wasn't originally the man to run with the joke torch. Another student had dressed up but he panicked and dropped it. Larkin, wearing a tie

Les Woodland

rather than a runner's vest, picked it up and started running.

Larkin said: "The only thing I could think about was what do I do when I get there. I just turned around and walked back down the steps, through the crowd and onto a tram and back to college."

The mayor saw best to treat it as a joke but the crowd was angry at being duped. It swirled as a mob on to the road and Hills had to appeal for calm. It took another police convoy to open a way for the flame-bearer and an army truck had to escort Bert Button.

And what happened to the plum-pudding can and the now extinguished underpants? They went to a reception at Sydney's city hall and ended up with a man called John Lawler, who kept them for years before growing tired of them and dropping them in the bin.

Five Things You Didn't Know You Didn't Know... About The Olympic Flame

1. The flame commemorates the day that Prometheus stole the gift of fire from the Greek god, Zeus.

2. Cash was so short in London in 1948 that gas firing the flame was turned down at night. Word spread that it had gone out. The organizers had to shrug off the cost and keep the flame turned high.

3. The flame for the 1976 Olympics in Montreal went out in the rain after the Games had started. An official relit it with a cigarette lighter. Horrified organizers put it out and used a back-up of the original flame.

4. The flame is lit at Olympia, original home of the Games, in the presence of 11 women representing the Vestal Virgins. It is lit by reflecting the light of the sun.

5. The first flame of the modern Olympics, at Amsterdam in 1928, was lit by a member of the city's electricity company.

6 (bonus!). The flame at the Tokyo Olympics of 1976 was carried by Yoshinori Sakai, a runner born on the day that the bomb fell on Hiroshima.

Les Woodland

43

How To Keep Virgins From Your Naked Body

The legend that athletes competed nude is true. The word "gymnasium", after all, comes from *gymnos*, the Greek for naked.

The story is that Orsippus was on his way to winning the stadium race in 720 BCE when his shorts fell down. There are suspicions, spread by a man called Pausanius, that he let them fall because that way he could run faster: "A naked man can run more easily than one girt."

Others certainly noticed and Acanthus the Spartan lined up for the *dolichus* (the 24-stadia event) with no clothes on at all and that's the way it remained for everyone else.

These things never being clear, another version is that far from winning, Orsippus got his loincloth tangled round his knees and fell over. Whichever the version, a brief flirtation with loincloths—you can see them in illustrations on ancient vases—was over. Men were ordered to exercise naked henceforth.

Women weren't allowed to watch the Games—they and slaves had to stand on the hill and see what they could manage—but not because of the nudity. Going naked was part of the true beauty to which Greeks aspired. Tales that virgins were allowed to watch, however, have been discounted. The one woman likely to have been admitted to the sacred ground of Olympia was the priestess of the goddess Demetra, Chamyne, who could have watched from an altar opposite the judges' stand.

The first Games had hints of what was to follow. Warring states forgot their troubles and came to take part, companies outdid each other in the help they gave for commercial advantage, competitors ate or drank anything they thought would make them better, and, far from being Simon Pure amateurs, the best made a fortune from prizes and sometimes lived at public expense.

The games were held from 776 BCE until the Christian Byzantine emperor, Theodosius I, banned them in 393 CE after 1,170 years. The early Christians didn't take the same view about the beauty of the body and the celebration of earthly perfection. They believed the body merely imprisoned the soul, the important part, and that it ought to given hard work and a minimum food so that it would die quicker and release the soul to heaven. They weren't a bundle of laughs, the early Christians.

Olympia itself suffered under the new ideas, from earthquakes, a fire, flooding and the invasion of barbarians. Theodosius pulled a lot down. Much of what remained disappeared beneath the ground or was hidden by undergrowth. The ruins weren't found until the 1700s, after which the French archaeologists who found them were expelled from the country. Then German searchers uncovered other large parts and the work continues to this day. The start and finish lines are still there, and the judges' seats, and some of the seating for 45,000 spectators.

The entrance is beyond the bridge over the Kladeos, signposted from the modern village. The gymnasium is there, and the restored wrestling school, the priest's house and the workshop where the massive statue of Zeus was sculpted. The altar where athletes swore the Olympic oath also survives. The most intact structure is the temple of Hera. Not having lost their sense of fun, the old Greeks mixed religious celebrations with orgies. Like we all want to do.

Five Things You Didn't Know You Didn't Know... About Bygone Olympics

1. The modern Olympics were started by Pierre de Coubertin but he had historical precedence in his native France, from the *Olympiade de la République,* run annually from 1796 to 1798.

2. Those 1796 games introduced metric measurements to sport, three years before they were adopted by France itself.

3. De Coubertin was inspired by sport in English private schools and by the Wenlock Olympian Games held in Shropshire, England, since 1850.

4. The English city of Liverpool held a Grand Olympic Festival annually from 1862 to 1867, although only for gentlemen.

5. The men behind the Wenlock Games and the festival in Liverpool jointly devised what became the international Olympic charter.

44

How To Party Right Out Of The Games

You'd somehow think that swimmers wouldn't be great drinkers, given the perils of their sport. But Eleanor Holm proved it wasn't true. And a bout of tippling so upset Avery Brundage, the dour head of the American team and later of the whole Olympics, that he threw her out of the 1936 Games before she even reached Europe.

As befits a woman said to boast that she trained on champagne, she died of liver failure. She was, to be fair, 90 or 91. Her exact age was something her family disagreed about.

Eleanor Holm was the world's star swimmer between the wars. She set world records in two distances at backstroke and won the gold medal at the Los Angeles Games in 1932. As she boarded the *Manhattan* in New York harbor on July 15, 1936, seven years had passed since she lost a race. She was the one person every backstroker feared at Berlin.

But long before the ship slipped within sight of the European mainland, Holm had been thrown out of the team. The news startled Americans used at the time to treating athletes like film stars and knowing nothing of their private lives. The journalists who'd been drinking with her that night didn't spare the details. It turned out that she was the only member of the team at a party on the first-class deck. That much suggests she wasn't supposed to be there in the first place. She'd been invited by two other passengers, the playwright Charles MacArthur and his wife, Helen Hayes.

Holm, it's true, didn't hide the glamor in her life. She had turned down a chance to join the Ziegfeld Follies. She was married to a band leader and danced for him in a white swimming suit, high heels and a cowboy hat. She was a party animal. She said of her time in Los Angeles: "I was hardly dry at those Olympics when I was whisked

Les Woodland

from one studio to another—Warner Brothers, MGM, Paramount—to take screen tests."

She did confess to a few drinks at a cocktail party on the second night at sea. But that understated it. She was found close to a coma. The team doctor called her an acute alcoholic. She said it wasn't so and blamed Brundage, hardly a bundle of fun, for not liking her.

She said: "This chaperone came up to me and told me it was time to go to bed. God, it was about 9 o'clock, and who wanted to go down in that basement to sleep anyway? So I said to her: 'Oh, is it really bedtime? Did you make the Olympic team or did I?' I had had a few glasses of champagne. So she went to Brundage and complained that I was setting a bad example for the team, and they got together and told me the next morning that I was fired. I was heartbroken."

Other reports say it was rather later than 9 PM. She was, they said, "helped back to her cabin" at six in the morning.

The team campaigned to have her reinstated but Brundage was firm. No. Holm hammered on Brundage's door. He wouldn't open it more than a crack. Through it, she wept her grief and begged to be allowed to swim. Brundage was unmoved. And her husband, Al Jarrett, wasn't impressed either. Her antics had embarrassed him, he said, and he wasn't struck on her affair with another man, either. They divorced.

She then married her lover, the impresario, Billy Rose. With him, she starred in 39 stage shows a week, along with two film Tarzans, Johnny Weissmuller and Buster Crabbe. Warner Brothers contracted her but resisted actually using her in a film. Rose and Holm divorced in 1954. The New York Times reported that the alimony came to $30,000 a year, plus $200,000 to be paid in 10-year lumps. It took her only a few months to marry an oil man, Tom Whalen. He died in 1984.

"All I did was drink a couple of glasses of champagne," she said years later. "I was married, singing in a nightclub with my husband's band. I was not exactly a child. It's not like I was hiding it."

She never forgave Brundage and she wept in the stands at Berlin as she watched the world's competitors parade without her. But she made the most of her time. She wrote—or had written for her—columns in American papers. She went to receptions given by Nazi leaders. Hermann Goering was so taken that he took a silver swastika from his uniform and gave it to her. When Holm married Billy Rose, who was Jewish, she had a copy made and put a diamond Star of David in the center.

"Being kicked off the team made me a bigger star than I really was," she said, saying her life in old age in Miami was playing cards and working for charities. "It's what all old ladies do," she said.

• • •

Controversy of a different sort ended the solo synchronized swimming in 1992. A Brazilian judge, Ana Maria da Silveira, pushed the wrong scoring button while Sylvie Fréchette of Canada was in the pool. But it was too late: the votes had been announced. Fréchette came second and the American, Kristen Babb-Sprague, won. There was an appeal but it didn't consult da Silviera. Fréchette was turned down. The row went on for more than a year. It ended when both swimmers received gold medals.

Les Woodland

45

How To Run Rings Round The Olympics

The winter Games have never been pure and straightforward. But nobody expected what happened at Salt Lake City in the USA in 2002. Because it simply paid selectors more and more until they agreed to give it the Games. It gave IOC members and their families more than $1 million in gifts and scholarships. The city was tarnished, America began a legal and political inquiry, and 10 IOC officials were thrown out.

Salt Lake City had long been keen on running the Olympics. But it failed every time it asked. In the end it became clear it would take something more. It would take, thought the men in charge—a lawyer, Tom Welch, and a car salesman, Dave Johnson—the sort of wining and dining that had gone on to secure the games for Nagano in Japan—a Games which Salt Lake had wanted.

Their first idea was to give IOC delegates a Stetson hat apiece. It wasn't much but it was a start. For 2002 delegates were offered perks that cost millions of dollars: ski trips, scholarships and even plastic surgery. They were sold land and buildings at less than cost and their family were given jobs. In 1995 the IOC said Salt Lake City had won.

All went well until December 10, 1998. Then Marc Holder, who represented Switzerland on the IOC, spotted the bribery. Welch and Johnson resigned and faced 15 charges of bribery and fraud, although they were cleared. Others in Salt Lake City stepped down, 10 members of the IOC were expelled and another 10 were disciplined. The selection committee was changed, limits were set for entertainment, and former Olympic athletes were brought in to the selection committee.

಄

The scandal brought other revelations. In Nagano, the regional governor said the city had secured the Games ahead of Salt Lake City thanks to millions of dollars in "illegitimate and excessive level of hospitality" including 4.4 million on entertainment alone. Holder, who broke the Salt Lake revelations, said there had been abuses in voting for Atlanta in 1996 and for Sydney in the 2000. He said four people "make a living out of this." The IOC had unknowingly been offering votes for between $500,000 and $1 million. The city winning the bid would be charged "something like three million to five million dollars."

The IOC president, Juan Antonio Samaranch, disassociated himself. He said "personal comments, are not official comments."

The chief organizer of Salt Lake City's bid, Frank Joklik, said: "I do not regard what was done as bribes even though I recognize that there have been perceptions contrary to that. I regret those perceptions. I don't think they are justified."

The former minister in charge of Sydney's bid said he was asked to offer bribes for votes but refused.

There was further criticism once the Games had started, but not of Salt Lake City's making. An assessment of the TV coverage offered to the world said: "NBC's style of coverage accelerated the trend of focusing on U.S. winners (of medals and endorsement contracts) while ignoring anonymous foreigners with hard-to-pronounce names (so much for the Olympics as a symbol of international peace and understanding). NBC seemed incapable of generating interest in non-U.S. athletes."

46

How To Snub Academia

Jamie Connolly dragged himself up from the slums of Boston—the big one in Massachusetts rather than the original on the English east coast. He did so well that he read classics at Harvard University just outside the city. He then became the first Olympic champion of the modern era—to the disdain of academia.

James Brendan Connolly won the triple jump, the first event of the Athens Games in 1896. And it cost him his place at Harvard. But his story goes back further.

Connolly was born in the USA of parents who had fled the hardship the Irish coast. He played in the street with other boys in the south of the city, went to school but never to high school. Instead, he left to work first as an insurance clerk and then in the American South with the army.

Like most Irishmen of the era, his parents were Catholic. They brought Connolly up in the same faith. In Savannah, Georgia, while with the army, Connolly joined the Catholic Library Association and helped form a football team. He joined the association's cycling club.

Pushing himself through society made him regret leaving school. He taught himself so successfully that in October 1895 he passed exams to study classics at Harvard. He would already have heard of the Olympic movement formed in Athens the previous year. And he was intrigued by the first Games to be held in 1896.

He asked Harvard permission to go and was refused. Connolly said he was told the only way was to resign. His recollection was that he said: "I am not resigning and I'm not making application to reenter. I'm getting through with Harvard right now. Good day!"

It may not have been so forthright. Connolly's memories, especially of paying or collecting funds for his own way to Athens (in reality his fare was paid largely by a sports club), are not always accurate. Harvard's records confirm that leave for Athens was declined but say Connolly then asked for an honorable withdrawal and was given it on March 19, 1896.

The truth, of course, could be somewhere between the two.

Connolly and other Americans taking part crossed the Atlantic on a German freighter. It stopped in Naples. There a thief grabbed his ticket for the rest of the journey but realized the lack of wisdom in robbing an Olympic athlete when Connolly chased after him and caught him. Connolly went by train to Athens and arrived three weeks after he had left America just as the Games were about to open.

Connolly, using a running style no longer allowed—two hops on the same foot—jumped 13.71 meters. He was a meter better than the next best and won the silver medal. Why silver? Because that's what winners were originally awarded. He then came second in the high jump and third in the long jump.

He returned to Boston a hero. But he never returned to Harvard. The university offered him an honorary doctorate but he refused. He went on to report on the Spanish-American war that secured Cuba for the USA and published hundreds of short stories and 25 novels. He also stood twice for Congress.

Les Woodland

47

How To Get Deeply Into Debt

What you do with everything you built for the Olympics is a problem that faces every city once the flame has gone out. Some leave things where they were, like the ski jumps and toboggan runs on the outskirts of Calgary. Some break them up, which is what happened to the wooden floor of the indoor arena in London in 1947. Finland had given it and London sold it, to a local builder. The money he paid covered the cost of the Argentine Olympic committee's check for £280, which bounced.

Montreal's problem was rather greater. Montreal had such a colossal debt after 1976 that it took three decades to pay it off. And that despite the predictions of the mayor, Jean Drapeau, that "the Olympics can no more have a deficit than a man can have a baby."

Long before the final bill was paid in December, 2006, the controversial stadium known as the Big O (for Olympic and for its donut shape) had become the Big Owe. Montreal was $1.5 billion in debt. Problems with the stadium and the retractable roof which never properly worked meant that work was finished after the Olympics had. That alone, with construction, repairs, renovation, debts and inflation, cost $1.61 billion.

Much was raised by taxing the city's smokers. Then Quebec banned public smoking and sales and tax dropped. It delayed clearing the debt by a further three months.

It is customary that every Olympics is preceded by gloomy tales of work falling behind, of stadiums not being finished in time. It is rare they ever come to anything. But in Montreal they were so bad right from the start that the Quebec provincial government felt obliged to take the project over.

Work was halted by a builders' strike and the retracting roof that was to have been the stadium's crown was left in a warehouse in

France until 1982. It was only in 1987 that it was added to the stadium. Only the following year did anyone manage to retract it. And then they found that it wouldn't retract if the wind blew at 40 kilometers per hour. When it did close, the atmosphere changed in the stadium and it rained indoors.

It was the second most costly stadium ever built.

Berlin held the Games only once but built a stadium twice. And both were kept in the family, the father—Otto March—designing the first and the son, Werner, the second. Only Werner's stadium ever saw the Olympics. Otto's *Deutsche Stadion* was to have been for 1916, Games that were canceled because of the first world war.

Werner's *Olympiastadion* was used in 1936.

The Germans planned originally to restore the 1916 stadium and use that 20 years later. Werner's son, Otto, March was given the job of tidying up what his father had created. Two years later the Nazis came to power and the old arena was neither big nor glorious enough. The Reich wanted something to outdo everyone. Down would come the old and up would go the new, still on the same site and with the lower structure 12 meters below ground level.

It had space for 110,000 plus one space, rather grander, designed for Hitler. The stadium's arch was to add drama to the arrival of the Olympic flame, carried from Athens that year for the first time. The idea came from one of Joseph Goebbels' advisers in the propaganda ministry.

Nobody ever mentioned what the stadium, those that surrounded it and the Games themselves cost the German state. The detailed accounts say that ticket sales gave a profit of a million Reichsmarks, the prewar currency. But the bill did not include money spent by Berlin and by the German state itself. Berlin's own figures showed it had spent 16,500,000 marks. The ruling Nazis never said what they had spent on behalf of the nation.

In the end the *Olympiastadion* survived the Hitler régime. It was liberated by the Russians, if a stadium can be liberated, at the price of only a scattering of machine gun bullets in its walls. It then became headquarters for the British occupying forces.

The *Olympiastadion* is one of the few surviving remains of prewar Olympic history and certainly its most extravagant. It was renovated

Les Woodland

in 2000 after a debate about whether it should be demolished to rid the city of its past, restored to make it of more use, or allowed to crumble as an ancient ruin. The soccer World Cup was held there in 2006—but not before workmen found an unexploded British bomb beneath the seats.

Marcel Schoenhardt photo

Five Things You Didn't Know You Didn't Know... About The Berlin Olympics

1. Claims that some teams gave the Nazi salute are still argued 80 years later. The Olympic salute, no longer used because it resembled that of the Nazis, also entailed raising a straightened arm at 45 degrees.

2. The policy of Hans von Tschammer und Osten, the sports minister in charge, was to use sport "to weed out the weak, Jewish and other undesirables."

3. The USA proposed boycotting Berlin rather than support the Nazis. They were persuaded to send a team by Avery Brundage, who said Jewish athletes were being treated fairly.

4. Pre-fascist Spain *did* stay away and tried to run a rival event, the People's Olympiad. Six thousand athletes from 22 countries entered but civil war started one day before it could begin.

5. China was voted to have the best anthem.

48

How To Upset A Lord

One of the central characters in the film, "Chariots of Fire", refused ever to watch it.

Lord David George Brownlow Cecil Burghley, a gold medalist in 1928, became president of the international Olympic movement and organizer of the Games in 1948. And why did he stay away? Because it showed another runner, Harold Abrahams, as the first to run round the Great Court at Trinity College, Cambridge, in the time it took the clock to toll 12 . It was a slight he never forgave. The depiction is a particular error because Abrahams had left Cambridge University four years earlier.

Burghley was a prickly character, a millionaire who placed full champagne glasses on the hurdles as he trained over them. His difficult nature persuaded the producers to portray him as Lindsay, a fictional character. Burghley had refused to allow his name to be used and the producers conceded, though there was no legal obligation. But denying him an eccentric achievement of which he was proud just made him worse.

Burghley's tiny running spikes and other memorabilia are on display in Burghley House, where he lived in northern Cambridgeshire, outside Stamford. Burghley House is where Herman Goering would have lived had the Germans occupied Britain.

Cambridge University doesn't appear in the film. The university worried it would suffer from association with anti-Semitism directed towards its former student, Harold Abrahams. The film's director, Harold Hudson, called his old school at Eton and the Cambridge scenes were filmed there, something the university later regretted.

There is a curious difference between the original film and the version distributed in the USA. The original shows a cricket match in the opening scenes. The American version deletes that and substitutes Abrahams and Aubrey Montague—who the film says attended Cambridge when in fact he went to Oxford—as they arrive at Cambridge by train. The change was inspired by American censorship. Not because cricket would be offensive to an American audience— puzzling, perhaps, but not obscene—but because it gave a chance for the two athletes to be sworn at by two resentful old soldiers on the platform. That single swear word lifted the film out of the "suitable for children" G rating, where the marketing people felt it would flop, and into the adult-but-safe PG category.

Eric Liddell, whom the film rightly shows as refusing to run the 100-meter heat because it was on a Sunday, became as famous after his death as he had been at his peak, thanks to the film.

He dropped the 100-meter when the timetable was published long before the Games—he didn't, as the film shows, find out only when boarding the ferry for France—and he ran the 400-meter in place of another team member. By then his religious devotion was widely known. When he went to the start, a masseur with the American team passed him a slip of paper. On it was a Biblical quotation: "Those who honor me, I will honor." Since the Americans were considered the favorites, this was a brave step.

It inspired Liddell and so did the hour of bagpipe music played by a Scottish band outside the stadium. He took the lead immediately but, instead of following convention by relaxing and just holding his advantage, he ran hard all the way. He won in an Olympic record of 47.6 seconds.

Liddell's career as an athlete soon ended. He spent a year at the Scottish Congregational College in Edinburgh, then returned to the London Missionary Society's mission in China, where he worked as a missionary from 1925 to 1943. He died of typhoid fever in Weishien, a Japanese internment camp, in 1945. The medals he won for the 400-meter and for coming third in the 200-meter were presented in May 1992 to his former university in Edinburgh.

Les Woodland

49

How To Take Defeat Badly

The pressure to win is enormous. It is bad enough to lose if you have spent a decade training. It can be intolerable if the weight of a nation is behind you. Nowhere, it seems, is this pressure greater than in Japan. To lose brings shame on a nation. The consequences can be tragic.

Take the marathon runner, Kokichi Tsuburaya, for instance. At 24, he took leave as a lieutenant in the Japanese Ground Self-Defense Group—the discreet name for the army—to run the marathon in Tokyo, his national capital. The marathon is an enthusiasm in Japan and crowds lined the route. A British runner recalled that he hadn't seen so many spectators since the Queen's coronation.

The world's best were there and they showed themselves from the start: Ron Clarke of Australia, the Irishman, Jim Hogan, and the winner in 1960, the Ethiopian, Abebe Bikila. The pace was high and Clarke, who was good when he could run alone but not when challenged, faded. He was passed by Kokichi Tsuburaya while, ahead, Bikila disposed of Hogan and ran alone into the stadium in a world record of 2 hours 1 minute 11 seconds.

Tsuburaya came into the stadium next to an accolade from the home crowd. Just behind, pressing him, was the British runner, Basil Heatley. Tsuburaya fought and struggled but it wasn't enough. Heatley passed him meters from the line.

Tsuburaya was humiliated. He should have won but he hadn't. He could have come second but he couldn't. He was third. It's said that the third man on the podium is often the happiest. But not Tsuburaya. He had shamed himself and his nation.

His apology was to train still harder, faster, longer. The result was a foot injury that wouldn't heal. He winced from lumbago. Surgeons operated but he couldn't run again for three months. It was too much.

ॐ

On January 9, 1968, never having overcome his shame, he slit his throat. The note that he left said: "I am too tired to run any more." His body, clutching his bronze medal, was found in his dormitory.

Nor was Abebe Bikila spared tragedy. He never ran again as he did in Tokyo. In 1968 a car crash 70 kilometers from Addis Ababa left him a paraplegic. He died of a brain hemorrhage in 1973 and was buried in the presence of the emperor, Haile Selassie, and 75,000 mourners.

As for Tsuburaya, a professor of sports philosophy in Japan said defeat is never an individual matter there. Those who lose face banishment from their group, he said, and by implication from society.

The magazine *Time* reported: "Understanding the culture in which Japanese athletes compete makes watching their defeats all the more painful. The agony of the gymnast, Naoya Tsukahara, whose hopes for an individual all-around medal were dashed when he inexplicably fell off the pommel horse, was obvious as he seemed to sleepwalk through his other events. His body was limp, his expression blank.

"'I didn't want to disgrace my nation', he said. Another young swimmer, Tomoko Hagiwara, climbed out of the pool after finishing seventh in her 200m individual-medley qualifying heat, her shoulders sagging, her head tilted downward.

"'What was the cause of your poor performance?' snapped a reporter for NHK, the national TV network. Hagiwara answered that she didn't shift smoothly between strokes and that her turns were poor.

"'Please remember those points and try to do better in the next race,' the reporter lectured."

• • •

It wasn't the runner who did badly in the Athens Games of 1896 but his butler. The Australian, Edwin Flack, won the 800- and 1,500-meter but worried about the marathon. What better, then, than have his butler ride beside him on a bicycle? He wouldn't be able to carry a tray but he could at least hand up bottles of water. Sadly, the aristocratic plan didn't work. Flack had no trouble but the butler collapsed.

Les Woodland

50

How To Put Glamor Into Ping-Pong

There's a man who writes for the *Washington Post* called Peter Carlson. And he described table tennis as "a goofy game that bored adolescents play in suburban basements until they lose the ball under the radiator."

Table tennis is one of the few sports in the world to have an odd name. Not "table tennis" itself, of course, but "ping-pong." Or, as it was called when British toffs invented first batted golf balls from one end of a table to the other with books, "wiff-waff." There's an even odder tale that it first saw life as "gossima", although that may have been the name on the box when a big London toy store began selling the means to play.

It was predictable that wiff-waff would die out. And no more was heard of gossima. But ping-pong was so respected a name that a British maker of bats and nets patented it in 1901. It was only to avoid breaching rights, and to prevent unnecessary publicity for a rival, that other companies called it table tennis. Now "ping-pong" is seen as faintly insulting, although the French for a male player is still *un pongeur* and, for a woman, *une pongeuse*.

Table tennis made it to the Olympics in 1988, a century after it was invented. It was so fast that television cameras couldn't keep up with it. The remedy was to make the ball bigger—40 millimeters rather than 38 millimeters—so it would catch the air and move more slowly. That suited television but it wasn't enough for less nimble players and a rival game has started, large-ball table tennis, with balls 44 millimeters across. It's seen as a big improvement by players who wear glasses.

The other change the sport made for Sydney was to scoring. Until then, the first player to score 21 points with a two-point lead won the game. That stretched the attention span of TV viewers, especially those who couldn't see the ball anyway. So table tennis opted for 11 points instead.

So far, so clear. But things are complicated, says Peter Carlson, by the players themselves. As he pointed out: "Jasna Reed, star player for the United States Olympic table tennis team, would like to clear up a couple of things about the romantic lives of big-time Ping-Pong players." Note that he follows a journalist's respect for trade names and spells it with capital letters. "First of all, she says, she is the ex-wife of only one of her teammates, not two. She never actually married Barney Reed. She merely took his last name back in the days when they were dating."

Reed used to be Jasna Fazlic. That was when she was Yugoslavian. It was as Fazlic that she came third in the doubles for Yugoslavia. She was still Yugoslavian for the next Games, in 1992, but by then she had become Jasna Lupulesku, having married a teammate.

Then Yugoslavia changed its name. It split into a handful of nations which then went to war with each other. Fazlic-Lupulesku-Reed had become Bosnia-Herzogonian. She gave up and went to Japan, then to America. In 2000 she played for the USA. But while love was still there for table tennis, it wasn't for a husband. They divorced.

Reed went back to her maiden name. But Americans aren't good at foreign names and they called her Miss Phallic. It's actually more like Fuzz-litch. She complained to her boyfriend, the American player Barney Reed, and he said he rather liked his own name and suggested Miss Phallic might enjoy it as well. So she went to court and became Jane Reed.

Reed hadn't been proposing marriage but that's what everyone assumed. In reality the relationship was short-lived. It was when they parted, and the table tennis world commiserated with both for a divorce which had never happened, they realized the second inconvenience to sharing a name.

She considered changing again but couldn't think of anything. She even asked for ideas in a magazine, the unconfusingly named *Table Tennis*, but they were as shortsighted as the folk who'd started playing with a 44mm ball. They couldn't think of anything that appealed. In

Les Woodland

the end, in 2009, she married the grand-sounding William H. Rather IV. She is now table tennis coach at a university in Texas.

Her old boyfriend, Barney Reed, says table tennis is "like martial arts combined with chess, the most exciting sport out there."

Fazlic-Lupulesku-Reed-Rather is more down to earth: "Look at old movies. Where do they play table tennis in movies? In jails and mental hospitals."

Fifty More Things You Didn't Know You Didn't Know

1. The American general, George Patton, took part in the modern pentathlon in 1912.

2. The Russian javelin thrower Elvira Ozolina was the best in the world. No woman had ever thrown further. But she was so disgusted by flopping in 1964 that she shaved off her hair.

3. Fanny Blankers-Koen won the 100-meter, 200-meter and the 80-meter hurdles and ran the last leg of the winning relay in London in 1948. The city of Amsterdam gave her a bicycle "so you won't have to run so much."

4. The Tanzanian marathon runner Richard Mbewa never got to the 1984 Olympics. A policeman saw him run by and assumed he was fleeing a crime. And shot him dead.

5. Anne Ottenbrite of Canada swam the 200-meter breaststroke in Los Angeles despite dislocating her right knee while showing off new shoes. She limped to the Games only to be in a car crash. She then strained her thigh while playing a computer game. And she still won the gold medal.

6. Briana Scurry, goalkeeper of the American soccer team, was so unsure of success in 1966 that she promised to run naked through the street if America won. Scurry kept to her word. It was at 2 AM and she ran just 10 meters, but she wore only her gold medal and a friend was there with a camera to prove it.

7. How many Olympic medalists played Tarzan? Count them: Johnny Weismuller won swimming golds in 1924 and in 1928; Buster Crabbe won a swimming bronze in 1928; Hermann Brix came second in the 1928 shot put; and Glen Morris won the decathlon in 1936.

Les Woodland

8. Alfred Krupp, who won in yachting in 1936 and also made that year's Olympic torch, is the only gold medalist to have been jailed for war crimes. He got 12 years for running Nazi armaments factories.

9. Shun Fujimoto broke his kneecap in the floor exercise in gymnastics in 1976. Whether Japan won the gold depended on how he performed next day. He was nearly faultless, without pain killers. He grimaced as his landing put pressure on his injured knee, held the position for the judges, then collapsed. Japan won.

10. Benjamin Spock, who wrote books about baby care, was a gold medalist in rowing in 1924.

11. The Swiss rower Gottfried Kottmann won the bronze in the single sculls on his 32nd birthday, 15 October 1964. Three weeks later, on 6 November 1964, he died in a car accident.

12. The Greek gymnast, Dimitrios Loundras, came second in the team parallel bars in Athens in 1896. He was 10 years 218 days old. He died aged 84.

13. There was unaccustomed class in the cycling road race near London in 1948 when officials were carried in a Rolls-Royce. The tone was lowered when two riders began fighting after falling off on a bend.

14. Wym Essajas was the pride of Suriname. Never until 1960 in Rome had anyone from his country taken part. Big things were expected in the 800-meter. But they never happened. Someone gave him the wrong starting time and he slept through his event. Eight years passed before Suriname fielded another Olympian.

15. Ingemar Johansson was disqualified in the final of the 1952 boxing for not "giving of his best." He returned to Sweden in shame. He then turned professional and flattened Floyd Patterson to win the world heavyweight championship of 1959. He finally received his Olympic silver medal in 1981.

16. Olympic gold medals aren't solid gold; they're silver with a thin coating of gold.

17. American featherweight Albert Robinson banged his opponent with his head in the 1968 boxing final. He was not allowed to receive a silver medal. The USA protested and he received it after he returned home.

The Olympics' 50 Craziest Stories

18. The American team, unhappy after crossing to Europe on an Army freighter, objected to the abandoned school they were to live in at Antwerp in 1920. The triple-jumper, Dan Ahearn, was thrown out—although reinstated—for finding somewhere else. The British settled in and borrowed kilts for a night of Scottish dancing.

19. The British diver D. F. Cane made such a mess of a double somersault in London in 1908 that he hit the water in a belly-flop. It hurt so much that he spent days in bed and missed the rest of the competition. Sweden, feeling sorry and recognizing his talent, gave him a silver cup.

20. Angelo Parisi won judo medals for both France and Britain.

21. Pierre de Coubertin, the father of the modern Olympics, pedaled around Paris on a tricycle to try to make the 1900 Games more popular.

22. The American, Irving Baxter, had to win the pole vault twice before judges in Paris in 1900 would make him the winner. His first jump was on a Sunday and his rivals protested they hadn't been able to take part because of religious convictions. Baxter's height was beaten when the event was rerun but the judges decided the original would count.

23. Water polo involves a lot of leaping about in the water and often a lot of illicit tugging and pulling when the referee can't see. Feel sympathy, therefore, for the Hungarian at the Games in Tokyo who bobbed to the surface without his trunks, watched by the whole of Japan on TV.

24. The Swedish wrestler Ara Abrahamian was so upset by a judging decision in 2004 that he left his bronze medal in the middle of the ring. He never got it back because the IOC took it away because he'd said the judges were bribed.

25. Lis Hartel of Denmark had to be lifted on and off her horse because of polio but she still won the silver medal in the 1952 dressage in Helsinki.

26. Judges announced a heat for third in the women's hurdles at Los Angeles in 1984. Then they watched films and placed only Kim Turner of the USA third. Michèle Chardeonnet of France left the ceremony in tears. Three months later the decision changed and she got her bronze medal.

Les Woodland

27. Hyman Miller, just 16, justified being favorite in the flyweight boxing in Amsterdam in 1928. The American seemed to win easily. But the judges picked Marcel Sartos of Belgium. Fighting began in the stands. The USA planned to withdraw its boxers in protest. The president of the US committee, Major General Douglas MacArthur, demanded they stay, saying: "Americans never quit."

28. Cliff Meidl carried the American flag at Sydney in 2000. In 1986, he came close to having both legs amputated after an electric shock 15 times more powerful than the electric chair. He was working in Los Angeles when he cut through three cables. The shock cracked his skull, ripped off two toes and burned him. Parts of his arm and shoulder were destroyed. He had 15 operations and spent three years on crutches before taking up kayaking to recover. Three years later he was in the Olympic team.

29. Belgium's team for football (scoccer) in 1921 was such an unpopular selection that the home crowd booed it in the final against Czechoslovakia. Fouls and arguments with the referee soured the game. The Czechs walked off and Belgium won in the absence of anyone on the field.

30. The Olympic Hymn was adopted in 1957. The English words are:

> *Immortal spirit of antiquity,*
> *Father of the true, beautiful and good,*
> *Descend, appear, shed over us thy light*
> *Upon this ground and under this sky*
> *Which has first witnessed thy unperishable fame.*
> *Give life and animation to those noble games!*
> *Throw wreaths of fadeless flowers to the victors*
> *In the race and in strife!*
> *Create in our breasts, hearts of steel!*
> *Shine in a roseate hue and form a vast temple*
> *To which all nations throng to adore thee,*
> *Oh immortal spirit of antiquity.*

31. Jay Nash McCrea, an American cyclist from Springfield, Illinois, must have wished he'd used his first rather than second name. He

knocked off so many other riders in the 1904 Games in St. Louis that he was known for ever more as Crash McCrea.

32. It was all very well, those Greeks of ancient times competing in the altogether. But times had changed by 1908 and American runners in London were told they'd be disqualified if they ran in white shorts.

33. Olympic budgets these days run to astronomical sums. The stadium at White City in London in 1908, though, cost just £44,000 to build. It held 66,000, so each seat came to about the price of a modern newspaper.

34. Which was all the more remarkable because the Games lasted from late April until the end of October, making the true cost of a seat around...well, work it out for yourself!

35. Sweden took the notion of neutrality to an extreme in 1912 when it refused to organize the boxing because it was against the law.

36. Ali Kazemi of Iran didn't even get as far as the fighting. He turned up for his boxing bout against Ashgar Muhammad in 1992 without his gloves. A second went running off to find them but got back outside the three minutes allowed to boxers once the fight is announced. The judges disqualified him.

37. The name Vola Ratsifandrihamanana was on everybody's lips in Barcelona when a phone call home to Madagascar revealed that soldiers had captured a radio station there and tried to overthrow the government. Neither she nor the island's swimming manager knew anything about it. And three hours later it didn't matter anyway because the soldiers were arrested.

38. To the great pleasure of sports broadcasters and typesetters, Vola Ratsifandrihamanana had a teammate called Mbolatiana Rasolofomanana.

39. The first person ever to cross the line in the modern Olympics was an American, Francis Lane, who won a heat of the 100m sprint in Athens in 1896. He tied for third in the final.

40. Bob Beamon was one of the few not to realize what he'd done. His record jump at Mexico was announced as 8.90 meters. That meant nothing and he stood bewildered as the crowd began to thunder. Americans use feet and inches and he had to ask for a

conversion—29'2½"—before he understood and collapsed from emotion.

41. Abebe Bikila, a member of Emperor Haile Salassie's imperial guard, was the first to win the marathon twice. But when he won the second, in Tokyo, he received his medal to the Japanese anthem because organizers couldn't find the Ethiopian one.

42. Nadia Comăneci (the final I is silent) was the first gymnast to receive a perfect score of 10, not just once but seven times in 1976. She always traveled with a little Eskimo doll from her collection of 200 dolls at home.

43. The opening oath is taken by a competitor and a judge, both from the host nation. The first was by the Belgian fencer Victor Boin in Antwerp in 1920. The competitor holds a corner of the Olympic flag as he swears: "In the name of all competitors, I promise that we shall take part in these Olympic Games, respecting and abiding by the rules that govern them, in the true spirit of sportsmanship, for the glory of sport and the honor of our teams."

44. The American fencer Joanna de Tuscan is said to have auditioned for "Gone with the Wind" but fled when she was shown to a casting couch. She was described at Berlin as "the most beautiful Olympian of the 1936 Games." She was thrown out of the fencing association when rivals from New York accused her of having her fare paid to a fencing demonstration.

45. Ron Clarke was asked two weeks before the 1956 Games to carry the Olympic flame. He was given a far larger torch to carry into the stadium itself, one that would spit flames and sparkle better on television. Unfortunately the sparks burned him and his shirt.

46. Abel Kiviat holds the record as the athlete to enjoy his medal longest. The American runner was 20 when he won a silver in the 1,500m at Stockholm on July 10, 1912. He died on August 24, 1991, aged 99—79 years and 45 days later.

47. The first flight of doves at the opening ceremony was at Athens in 1896. It became officially part of the day in 1920.

48. The horse events for Melbourne in 1956 were held in Stockholm. Australia wouldn't let the horses in because of quarantine laws.

49. Russia was so sure it would win the unofficial points competition in Helsinki in 1952—scoring for medals—that it built a scoreboard to show its superiority. Then Americans had a late run of successes and the Russians began demolishing it rather than be shown up. A press report was headed: "Russia caught with points down."

50. Myer Prinstein finished second in the 1900 long jump in Paris despite not even making the final. Prinstein, an American student who was Jewish, agreed with others not to compete on Sunday, the Christian Sabbath. His qualifying jumps were good enough for second.

Les Woodland